Dedication

For my mother
Clara Mayfield
who has walked beside me
every step of the way

and

For my husband
Roger Cawthon
who believed in me
and
loved me back to life

For now we see through a glass, darkly;
but then face to face: now I know in part; but then
shall I know even as also I am known.
And now abideth faith, hope, Love, these three;
but the greatest of these is Love.
—1 Corinthians 13:12–13

Getting Out

An Escape Manual for Abused Women

by Kathy Cawthon

Huntington House Publishers

Huntington House Publishers
P.O. Box 53788
Lafayette, Louisiana 70505

Library of Congress Card Catalog Number
95-75954
ISBN 1-56384-093-6

Printed in the U.S.A.

I am all the daughters of my father's house,
and all the brothers, too.
—from *Twelfth Night*
by William Shakespeare

If you bring forth what is within you, what you bring
forth will save you. If you do not bring forth what is
within you, what you do not bring forth will destroy you.
—St. Thomas Logian

The most important thing is to write in your own blood.
—Joni Mitchell

What Others Have Said about *Getting Out*:

Getting Out speaks right to the battered woman in terms she can understand. It's a comprehensive guide to identifying battering and escaping the violence. Any person who has ever thought "maybe this relationship isn't right" needs to read this book.

—Amy Wheeler, M.Ed.,
Battered Women's Counselor

It's "Everywoman's" worst nightmare—feeling stuck in a relationship with an abusive partner. From the pen of a woman who has been there, this book tells you how to get "unstuck" and get out. Whether you're planning to leave for the first time or the last time, make this book your guide. Copies of *Getting Out* should be for sale at every grocery check-out counter, and a copy should be included in the cost of a marriage license—as a kind of marital insurance policy.

—Carole Stoltz, C.S.A.C., L.P.C.

Most of us have dreams of the kind of lives we want to have when we grow up. Many women who have been victims of physical violence and verbal, emotional, and financial abuse in their intimate relationships forget what their dreams for themselves were, and eventually cannot even envision what their lives were like before the pain began. *Getting Out* should help women realize that there can be a life outside of the abusive relationship and give them the strength to awaken from the nightmare and start to build bright new dreams for the future.

—Cheryl Guidry Tyiska,
Director of Victim Services,
National Organization for Victim Assistance

Contents

Preface

When, as a little girl, I complained to my mother of vague aches and minor discomforts, she often told me they were growing pains. I remember thinking how glad I would be when I stopped growing. Little did I understand then that growth was not something that would end when I reached my adult height.

We continue to grow throughout our lives and until our lives end, and that growth often brings growing pains. Every experience, good or bad, is an opportunity for growth; what we choose to do with that opportunity is up to us.

Being in an abusive relationship is one of the worst experiences a woman can have, and leaving an abusive relationship is one of the hardest decisions a woman can make. Getting out means making major life changes, and change does not come easily, especially when we find we must change ourselves. Change is almost never without pain and risk, but the rewards can be enormous if that change is seen as an opportunity for growth. The growing pains will come, but they will go away, too.

I know this because I've been there. I know how hard it is to open yourself up to the possibility that you are in an abusive relationship. I know how hard it is to leave someone with whom you have a long, intense history, especially when he is looking you in the eye and pleading with you to stay because "it will never happen again." I know what it is to be terrified of leaving and terrified of staying and to not know for sure which is worse. I know what it is to believe you can't live without him, even though a tiny voice inside you keeps telling you that you must.

Please listen to your own voice. Approximately four thousand women die each year because they didn't listen to themselves and they didn't seek help from the people who could have advised and counseled them. Approximately four million women are physically assaulted by their partners every year, and millions more are subjected to verbal attacks so debilitating that it is only a matter of time before their abusers become physical in their battering.

When I escaped my abuser, there were no battered women's shelters or hotlines to call. I made many mistakes, and went backwards more times than I like to think about. But, I made it and have never regretted my decision to leave.

In the wake of the Nicole Brown Simpson and Ron Goldman murders, the subject of domestic violence has received incredibly widespread attention in the media. When I began to see and hear the statistics relating to annual injuries and deaths resulting from domestic violence, I was dumbfounded. Realizing that shelters for battered women and hotlines are available almost everywhere now, I was puzzled as to why women weren't taking advantage of these lifelines.

It didn't take me long to figure it out. There are as many reasons as there are abused women, but they can all be reduced to one: they don't get out because they don't know how to take the first steps, which are admitting they are abused and asking for help. These are scary steps to take alone.

When I looked to see what information was available in book form to women who were considering taking these steps, I found next to nothing written for the *victims*. I found lots of material written for counselors and therapists who specialize in treating battered women. I found volumes of statistics and definitions worded so that no one but researchers and statisticians could understand them. And, I found an abundance of material for attorneys and legal advocates. The one or two books I found that might have helped a victim of abuse to examine her situation and make some decisions were grossly outdated, and even they were a bit too clinical to be easily read and understood.

This book is written for *you*. You who are wondering, "What is 'abuse' and how do I know if that word applies to me?" You who are telling yourself, "I know this relationship is abusive and I should get out, but I'm scared and I don't know how." You who are telling yourself, "Last night was the last time. He promised. It won't happen again."

In these pages you will find clear definitions and straightforward advice. You will also find inspirational quotations, prayers, and poetry that have helped me along my own journey. I hope you will find the answers you are looking for and the courage to make changes, even though those changes may be painful. Remember that the pain means you are growing.

This book is intended to be a bridge from your house to the outside world where you will find the people who will help you and people who will care about you, where you will one day find the peace and joy you so richly deserve, and where, ultimately, you will find yourself again.

Now you can take the first steps and cross that bridge. You are not alone.

Peace and prayers,
Kathy Cawthon

Acknowledgments

I am deeply indebted to the many individuals who were instrumental in the completion of this project. Sincere thanks go to all those who work in the interest of abused women and children through programs, shelters and private practices around the country, who shared their materials with me, returned all my phone calls and answered all my questions; to Amy, Tom, Carole and Anne, who provided valuable professional input and insight; to "My-Friend-Kathy," whose technical wizardry kept my computer and me humming along in sync and who has never been more than a phone call away in good times and in bad; and to my terrific family, who really pitched in to help me deliver this project on time.

Introduction

How ironic that domestic violence, a crime that has been around since ancient times, would suddenly be catapulted into the minds and mouths of all people because of the trial of O.J. Simpson, an athletic superstar. Whatever the reason, those of us who have worked in this area of crime for decades are grateful that domestic violence is finally coming out of the shadows.

Kathy Cawthon writes with credibility and clarity as only a survivor can. She writes about her survival of this crime which victimizes millions each year while both traumatizing its current victims and breeding generations of future abusers. She tells her personal story of growing up in a household drenched in the powerful yet insecure personality of her abusive father, a man obsessed by ferocious power and control issues. Growing up under the domination of such a personality made it more likely that she would marry someone like her own cruel father.

Cawthon's message is straightforward and honest: that while the criminal justice system has made some progress in the area of domestic violence, there is still a long way to go; that community, family, and one's usual support systems cannot be relied on for much help in cases of domestic violence; that there are not enough shelters for battered women and children; and that victims of domestic violence must now and for the foreseeable future ultimately rely on themselves.

Getting Out: An Escape Manual for Abused Women provides direction and answers to the questions victims of domestic violence have about safety issues and available resources, and it offers meaningful and serious guidelines for recognizing the dynamics and symptoms of potential power and control junkies. It is a "must read" for every woman who finds herself on the victim-end of "domestic terrorism," the beaten, the browbeaten, the neglected, the overwatched . . . the ones who walk on eggshells.

—Sgt. Anne O'Dell

Sergeant O'Dell works in the Domestic Violence Investigations Unit of the San Diego Police Department. She is the training director of the program for Specialized Training on Preventing Domestic Violence.

*No man is an island, entire of itself; every man is a piece
of the Continent, a part of the main . . . any man's death
diminishes me, because I am involved in Mankind.*

—John Donne

A Prayer for Faith
by Margaret Sangster

*God, give me back the simple faith that I so long have clung to,
    My simple faith in peace and hope, in loveliness and light—
Because without this faith of mine, the rhythms I have sung to
    Become as empty as the sky upon a starless night.*

*God, let me feel that right is right, that reason dwells with reason,
    And let me feel that something grows whenever there is rain—
And let me sense the splendid truth that season follows season,
    And let me dare to dream that there is tenderness in pain.*

*God, give me back my simple faith because my soul is straying
    Away from all the little creeds that I so long have known;
Oh, answer me while still I have at least the strength for praying,
    For if the prayer dies from my heart I will be quite alone.*

God is our hope and strength: a very present help in trouble.

—Prayer Book, 1662

*When pain is to be borne, a little courage helps more than much
knowledge, a little human sympathy more than much courage,
and the least tincture of the love of God more than all.*

—C. S. Lewis

Chapter One

You Are Not Alone

First, the Bad News

I have good news and bad news for every woman who has ever been abused or who is not sure but thinks she might have been abused in the past or might be in an abusive relationship now. Let's start with the bad news.

The bad news is that you are not alone. Whether you are a teen-ager struggling to overcome the trauma of childhood sexual abuse, a newlywed whose husband hits you, or an older woman whose husband has you convinced you are crazy because you are fearful of him and depressed, there are millions of women throughout this country and the world who share your heartache and terror. The statistics, while horrifying, only begin to tell the story.

- A woman is beaten every fifteen seconds in this country. Some experts say it is now every nine seconds.
- Four million women in the United States are physically assaulted every year by their domestic partners. That number represents more women than are injured annually in muggings, rapes, and automobile accidents combined.
- Approximately one in three women who report to emergency rooms are treated for injuries resulting from domestic violence.

• Millions more are verbally abused and systematically demoralized and humiliated by their partners, which often results in their being chronically depressed and suicidal. One in four women who commits suicide was the victim of domestic violence.

• Of these millions of abused women, approximately four thousand die each year at the hands of their abusers. *Eight to ten die every day.* More than half of female homicide victims were killed by their male partners.

• The American Medical Association reported in 1992 that as many as one in three women will be a victim of domestic violence in her lifetime.

• Also in 1992, the U.S. Surgeon General's Office reported that physical abuse by male partners had become the leading cause of injuries to women ages fifteen to forty-four.

The other part of the story is, of course, that each of these numbers is so much more than a figure on a data sheet or a line on a graph. Each number represents a person, a woman with a name and a birthday, a beautiful face with eyes of blue or brown or green, a characteristic way of walking, a voice that sounds like no one else's. Each number is just a symbol for a human being with a favorite breakfast cereal, a favorite color, a jacket or sweater that makes her feel good, a song she likes to sing with her children. Unfortunately, each one also has (or had) someone in her life who occasionally brings her joy, but who more often causes her intense trauma and terror. And, every mark in the tally of victims of domestic violence not only represents the shattered life of a living, breathing woman, but also the countless grieving hearts of the children, parents, grandparents, other relatives, and friends who love these women.

If you are currently in a violent relationship or are suffering the aftermath of a past relationship that was abusive, you may find some small measure of comfort in knowing that you are not alone. You have many millions of "sisters" who endure every day the same heartache, fear, and physical pain you are facing. When you pray for yourself and your children, pray for them and theirs, too.

The Good News

Now for the good news. The good news also is that you are not alone! Nearly two thousand programs throughout the United States—programs that didn't exist even a few years ago—provide a wide variety of services to battered women and their children. Most large communities have at least one shelter for battered women and their children, and some smaller communities have resource facilities such as cooperating hotels and "safe houses," private homes whose owners offer to provide temporary emergency shelter. Every state now has a domestic violence hotline that can be accessed twenty-four hours a day, 365 days a year. Appendix B at the end of this book lists those numbers by state.

Police and sheriff's departments around the nation are conducting training sessions to better equip their staffs to diffuse violent domestic situations. Every state has passed or is currently working to enact legislation to ensure victims of domestic violence the protection they need and deserve. In chapter 3, we will look at some of the problems within the legal system— and some of them are quite serious—but overall the courts and police departments throughout the country are making an effort to protect the victims of domestic violence.

This book is part of the good news, too. If you are unsure whether you are in an abusive relationship, if you have not yet confided to another human being that you are being abused, even if you think you have no one to talk to (you do; you just haven't met them yet—keep reading!), you now have this book in your hands. It will become your best friend until you connect with the people who will help you. It will guide you every step of the way from determining whether you are in an abusive relationship (and, because you have picked up this book and are reading it, I can almost guarantee that you are or that you know someone who is) through the steps you need to take in order to escape your abuser and all the way to finding your sanity again, getting on with your life and letting go of your painful past.

Some Basic Terms

More of the good news is that domestic violence now has a name. Children and women have been abused by the men in their lives throughout history, but many abusive behaviors were not recognized or identified as cruel or excessive. From earliest times, it was considered the right—even the duty—of parents to beat disobedient or lazy children, of masters to whip servants, slaves, and apprentices for real or imagined wrongs, and of husbands to discipline and punish wives who weren't appropriately subservient. Society accepted these behaviors as normal. If something is considered normal, it's not a subject of conversation. And, if people don't talk about it, it doesn't need a name.

Some of the terms used in discussions of domestic violence are interchangeable, while others are specific to age and sex. The term *domestic violence* itself includes any kind of violent, aggressive, or cruel treatment by a member of a household against another member of the same household, including but not limited to the violent person's children, spouse, and other relatives. Domestic violence includes abusive treatment of the elderly by their children, grandchildren, and other household members; it also includes abusive treatment of parents and siblings by teen-agers and adult children living in the home. That treatment may include but is not limited to physical battering (pushing, hitting, slapping, beating, etc.), verbal abuse (name-calling, verbal threats, insults, etc.), and sexual assault.

Wife beating refers to physically assaultive behaviors against the abuser's female spouse, while *wife abuse* and *wife battering* are broader terms which refer to both verbal and physical assaults (although some experts reserve the word *battering* to refer specifically to incidents of physical abuse). *Spouse abuse* likewise covers both physical and verbal abuse, but recognizes the fact that husbands can be and are abused by their wives. (While this book is specifically written for women who are in abusive relationships with men, it is not the author's intent to ignore or deny the existence of other abusive relationships among adults. Readers who are in such relationships will find that most of the material presented here applies to their situations as well.)

For the purposes of this book, "abuse" and "battering" are used to refer to the physical, emotional, psychological, or sexual mistreatment of a woman by her male partner. All of the information in this book applies to teen-age girls as well; they are just as vulnerable to and likely to be involved in abusive "romantic" relationships as older women. (If you are a parent, relative, or friend of a teen-age girl who is in an abusive relationship, you will find helpful information in chapter 10.)

Domestic Violence through the Ages

As stated earlier, women and children have been the victims of violent treatment at the hands of the men who claim to love them throughout history, but this treatment was not recognized as cruel or abusive until fairly recently. Harsh treatment of those smaller or weaker or in a lower social position has been generally accepted for many centuries and even now is

often seen as a source of humor. Who hasn't seen a
cartoon drawing of a caveman with a club in one hand,
dragging a woman by the hair with the other? While
this caricature may or may not be historically accurate,
it certainly represents as humorous the infliction of
pain and forced submission on a woman.

Syndicated cartoons such as "The Lockhorns,"
"Beetle Bailey," and "Andy Capp" rely heavily on the
use of insults, put-downs, deceitful actions, lying, and
fighting between spouses to effect what the cartoonists
and their fans apparently consider humorous. The fact
that millions of readers enjoy these cartoons says that
we as a society still accept these behaviors as normal in
domestic situations.

Most people are familiar with the expression "rule
of thumb," which is any generally accepted measure-
ment such as your foot being approximately a foot
long and the distance from your nose to the end of
your outstretched hand being about a yard. What most
don't realize, however, is that the expression has been
handed down through the centuries from its origin in
European Common Law which stated that a man could
beat his wife as long as he used a rod no thicker than
his thumb.

(Information Plus, a research and information service in Wylie, Texas, publishes biennially an updated
report entitled *Domestic Violence: No Longer Behind the
Curtains*. Much of the following historical information
is from the 1993 edition of that report, and the 1995
edition—available from Information Plus by the time
this book is published—is recommended reading for
all professionals in the field of domestic violence and
for students who intend to work in this field. The
service's address is listed at the end of this book under
"Other Resources.")

Countless historical documents endorse wife beating and give instructions for administering such "dis-

cipline" correctly. The *Rules of Marriage* drawn up by Friar Cherubino of Sienna, Italy, in the fifteenth century stated the following:

> When you see your wife commit an offense, don't rush at her with insults and violent blows, rather, first correct the wrong lovingly. (If this doesn't work) scold her sharply, bully and terrify her. And if this still doesn't work . . . take up a stick and beat her soundly. It is better to punish the body and correct the soul than to damage the soul and spare the body. . . . You should beat (her) . . . only when she commits a serious wrong. . . . . Then readily beat her, not in rage, but out of charity and concern for her soul.

English law condoned the practice of wife beating until the early nineteenth century, at which time a husband's right to chastise his mate in this manner was removed officially from the law books but, of course, the practice continues to this day in England just as it does throughout the world.

American law derived from English law, thus, the right of a husband to beat his wife was accepted in the New World from its earliest days. However, husbands were advised by the courts to administer such beatings with discretion and only after other methods of discipline had proven ineffective.

The North Carolina Court ruled in 1864 in the *State v. Jesse Black* as follows:

> A husband is responsible for the acts of his wife and he is required to govern his household, and for that purpose the law permits him to use towards his wife such a degree of force as is necessary to control an unruly temper and make her behave herself; and unless some permanent injury be inflicted, or there be an excess of violence, or such a degree of cruelty as shows that it is inflicted to gratify his own bad pas-

sions, the law will not invade the domestic fo-
rum, or go behind the curtain. It prefers to
leave the parties to themselves, as the best mode
of inducing them to make the matter up and
live together as man and wife should.

It was not until 1871 that American men were
denied by law the right to beat their wives. In *Fulgham
v. The State*, an Alabama court ruled as follows:

A rod which may be drawn through the wed-
ding ring is not now deemed necessary to teach
the wife her duty and subjection to the husband. The husband is therefore not justified or
allowed by law to use such a weapon, or any
other, for her moderate correction. The wife is
not to be considered as the husband's slave.
And the privilege, ancient though it be, to beat
her with a stick, to pull her hair, choke her, spit
in her face or kick her about the floor, or to
inflict upon her like indignities, is not now acknowledged by our law.

The "privilege" isn't acknowledged—and hasn't
been for 125 years!—but battering still happens to
nearly 30 percent of all women in relationships with
men and to 25 percent of all pregnant women in relationships. The "privilege" isn't acknowledged, but
battering is now the most common source of injury to
women. The "privilege" isn't acknowledged, but four
million women require the attention of medical personnel or police officers because of domestic violence
every year, and thousands of these women die.

We Are Not Alone

Violence against women by their male partners is
a universal reality and a global tragedy. Wife beating
is accepted in most Middle Eastern countries; women
raised in these countries are culturally and religiously

indoctrinated to accept these beatings and other demeaning treatment as part of their lot in life.

Female circumcision, the ritual sexual mutilation of young girls' genitalia, has been performed on more than 80 million African women according to the World Health Organization, and the practice is also common in some parts of the Middle East. This cruel surgery is carried out during tribal ceremonies without benefit of sterile procedures or anesthetic. Many of the girls suffer severe blood loss, shock and infection, and some die during or after the procedure. Because sex for the survivors is uncomfortable at best, but more often excruciatingly painful, the men maintain total control over their daughters' and wives' sexual lives. A daughter who has been so mutilated is not likely to be promiscuous and, as a wife (men in these countries will not marry a woman who has not been circumcised), she will most certainly be faithful.

Some other horrors endured by women around the world include the following:

• The practice of burning to death a bride whose dowry is unsatisfactory is common in India (more than 690 in New Delhi in one year; nearly 1000 in another year in the state of Gujurat).

• In Brazil, a man can literally get away with murder if he can elude capture for three days after killing his wife.

• Baby girls often go without food, medical treatment, and other basic care in many Asian countries where male children are highly prized. Where food, water, and medicine are in limited supply, baby girls are often left to die.

• Chinese and Indian women rely on medical tests to determine the sex of their unborn children. Female babies are frequently aborted.

Heard enough? There is much more. The following information is taken from *A National Crime Vic-*

timization Survey Report published by the U.S. Department of Justice, Bureau of Justice Statistics, in January of 1994.

- In France, 95 percent of all victims of violence are women, 51 percent of these at the hands of their husbands.
- In Denmark, 25 percent of women cite violence as the reason for divorce.
- Domestic violence is present in at least 70 percent of Mexican families, but most cases go unreported.
- In some areas of Papua, New Guinea, 67 percent of wives have experienced domestic violence in their marriages.
- Over two-thirds of women in Korea are beaten regularly by their husbands.
- In Nicaragua, 44 percent of men admit to having beaten their wives or girlfriends regularly.
- At least 50 percent of all married women in Thailand experience domestic violence.

Still Feeling Alone? Read On!

All of these numbers are important in helping us to understand that we are not alone. Still, as you read this, you may be thinking, "All of that is horrible, but how does it help me? How can I identify with some poor woman in Thailand or New Guinea?" You also may be tempted to think, "Burned to death? Sexually mutilated? I guess I should count my blessings that my husband only beats me/verbally humiliates me/yells at me and blames me for everything/forces me to have sex with him."

Knowing how many millions of women throughout the world endure terror, heartache, and physical torment at the hands of their current or former husbands or boyfriends every day can help you in two ways: it can help you admit that you are in an abusive relationship, and it can help you to feel less alone. Many women who are being abused feel ashamed of their situation and try very hard to keep it a secret. For these women, learning that millions of other women are treated exactly the same way by their partners and that this treatment is called *abuse* serves as a wake-up call. You don't need to memorize the statistics, but keep the general idea in mind as you begin to plan your journey to recovery from the violence in your life. Remember, you are not alone, and you have never been alone.

Remember, too, that the good news is you never will be alone in dealing with the abuse because you are going to begin right now to plan your escape, and, in so doing, you are going to meet many caring people who will help you on your way. Many of those people have been where you are right now, and they have been where you are going. Begin today preparing yourself to meet them, trust them, and learn from them.

As for thinking your situation is any less serious than any other woman's anywhere else in the world, stop that right now! If you remember nothing else from having read this chapter, memorize these simple words: *Love doesn't hurt*. If the man who claims to love you is hurting you in any way, his "love" is a lie.

Me, Too

I spent the first thirty years of my life in households where abuse of one kind or another was frequent fare. Today, more than twelve years after getting out, I am living proof that *you can get out and you can live a life free of violence*. Take these words to heart: Life is beautiful. God is good. You will be happy again.

Sticks and stones may break our bones,
but words will break our hearts.
—Robert Fulghum

The pain of the mind is worse than the pain of the body.
—Publilius Syrus

He healeth those that are broken in heart.
—The Book of Common Prayer

A Man
by Nina Cassian

While fighting for his country, he lost an arm
and was suddenly afraid:
"From now on, I shall only be able to do things by halves.
I shall reap half a harvest.
I shall be able to play either the tune
or the accompaniment on the piano,
but never both parts together.
I shall be able to bang with only one fist
on doors, and worst of all
I shall only be able to half hold
my love close to me.
There will be things I cannot do at all,
applaud for example,
at shows where everyone applauds."

From that moment on, he set himself to do everything with
    twice as much enthusiasm.
 And where the arm had been torn away
a wing grew.

Chapter Two

Me, Too

The Great Gorilla Hunt

When I was about six years old, a neighborhood bully told me a giant gorilla had escaped from the zoo and that it was going to eat me alive in my bed that night. It never occurred to me to question the truth of his story. I believed every word of it and was terrified.

That night I lay sobbing into my pillow and waiting for what I believed to be my inevitable end at the hands of some great hairy monster. My father heard me crying and came into my room. He sat down on my bed, took me in his arms, and asked me what was wrong. I told him about the gorilla. He didn't laugh or tell me I was being silly. He didn't tell me that gorillas don't eat people or that there was no zoo within several hundred miles of where we lived. He wore a serious expression as he took me by the hand and led me into the kitchen. He handed me a flashlight, hoisted me up onto his shoulders, and together we went out into the night to search for the gorilla.

That was a magical night in my childhood. I felt like a courageous hunter, strong and smart. Together my father and I searched the neighborhood. I shone my flashlight between the houses, behind garbage cans, up into the trees, and everywhere else I thought a gorilla on the run might hide. We looked until I was satisfied there was no gorilla. My father took me home and tucked me back into bed with the flashlight as added security. I went to sleep feeling safe and powerful.

The memory of that night is remarkable for another reason, too. It is the only detailed memory I have of time spent with my father during which I felt loved and safe. There are a few other good memories, but they are tiny fragments: of him dancing with me when I was very small, my feet on top of his; of his believing me once when I was in trouble and no one else believed me; of him saying I made the best french fries he had ever tasted.

Most of what I remember of time spent with my father is not just distinctly unhappy, but also terrifying and dangerous.

An educator by profession, my father had extensive training in education, psychology, and child development, and he held several postgraduate degrees. No one who knew him in a professional capacity would ever have believed what our lives were like at home.

It would be more than twenty-five years before I would learn two very important facts about abusers which applied to my life at that time: that domestic violence knows no cultural, educational, economic, racial, or religious boundaries, and that abusers are not abusive all the time.

My father's behavior was, at best, unpredictable; at worst, wildly erratic and irrational. That absence of consistency is what I remember most clearly because it was the most frightening aspect of his personality. A comment or event which caused him to smile one day could send him into a rage the next. My mother, brother, and I never knew when the next outburst would occur or where the next blow would land. When my mother and I speak of those times today, we refer to them as the days when we "walked on eggshells."

A Broken Record

When I was about eight or nine years old, my parents and brother and I went to a cookout at the home of friends. Several families had gathered for the party. The dozen or so young adults sat on lawn chairs or stood in small groups, sipping cocktails or beers and chattering about jobs, children, and current events.

Toddlers and small children played hide-and-seek among their mothers' legs and squealed as they darted in and out around the yard. I was one of three older children (a boy and two girls) who went into the house to escape the antics of the younger children and the boredom of the grownups' conversations.

The boy was the son of the party's hosts. He invited the other girl and me into his room to play records. We spread his collection of 45s across the bed to better see the choices. After putting a record on to play, I sat down on a corner of the bed—and on a record. The plastic disk snapped in half. Before I could stammer out an apology, the boy ran crying to his parents in the back yard.

As he raced from the room, my embarrassment turned to terror. *No, please, don't go out there*, I tried to call to him, but only a whisper came out. *I'll tell my mother later and she'll buy you a new record, just please, please don't go out there. You don't know what he might do to me.*

But the boy was gone. I froze and waited, my heart pounding on my ribcage. There was no way to know whether this was something my father would dismiss as unimportant or something that would send him into a rage.

Then my father was there in the doorway along with my mother and the parents of the boy. The host and hostess made light of the situation and told their son to stop making such a fuss. My mother said, "I'm sure it was an accident. We'll replace the record, won't

we, Kathy?" I nodded silently. My father said nothing,
only stared at me with the cold smile that told me my
fear of what he might do was valid, that my punishment for this embarrassing display of carelessness would
be severe.

He hung back until the other adults had gone back
outside, then took my upper arm firmly in his hand
and drew me into the hallway. Still smiling, he said,
"Wait 'til I get you home." My arm burned as he walked
away to rejoin the party.

Every minute of the remainder of the evening crept
by. I couldn't eat. Several of the women spoke quietly
to me, telling me not to be embarrassed about the record
and urging me to eat. But, a knot of terror filled the
void where an appetite should have been. Every time
my eyes met my father's, he smiled at me.

It was late when we headed home in the car. My
parents chatted up front. My brother fell asleep beside
me on the back seat. I sat quietly, knowing what was to
come. My stomach hurt and, in spite of the warmth of
the midsummer Texas night, my hands were cold.

When we got home, my father told me to go into
the bathroom and wait for him there. I did as I was
told. As I stood in shorts and shirt with my bare feet
on the cold tile floor, my knees shook so badly I had
to sit down on the toilet. I kept thinking, *Don't spank
me, Daddy. Please, Daddy, don't.*

My father came into the bathroom and shut the
door behind him. He told me to stand on the toilet
seat and turn my back to him. He removed his belt,
doubled it and began beating the backs of my bare
legs.

He spoke one word with each blow: "I . . . have . . . never
. . . been . . . so . . . embarrassed . . . in . . . my . . . life.
. . . Stop . . . crying. . . . Why . . . don't . . . you . . . look.
. . . Don't . . . you . . . dare . . . cry . . . where . . . you're
. . . sitting. . . . Shut. . . . up . . . this . . . minute. . . . I

. . . will . . . stop . . . spanking . . . you . . . when . . . you
. . . stop . . . crying."

My father did not yell or scream when he was
beating us. His voice was an eerie monotone, the vol-
ume low. And always there was that command to stop
crying, the reminder that the beating would end only
when I stopped crying. The message was clear: I was
responsible for my own pain.

Breathing Lessons

I stopped crying by going someplace else in my
mind and willing myself to stop breathing. Sometimes
I went to the rope swing in my grandparents' yard or
to the lake where my grandfather took me fishing,
sometimes just to a blank place inside my head where
I couldn't feel anything. (Psychologists use the term
dissociation for this phenomenon which is a sort of self-
defense mode the conscious mind goes into in order
to escape great pain. It is an important and well-known
survival mechanism frequently observed in abused
children and in adults who were abused as children.
There are degrees of severity of the disorder, of course,
the worst being the phenomenon known as multiple
personality disorder.) When I did this, I could stop
crying. When I stopped crying, my father stopped
beating me. Just that and nothing more. He just
stopped, and then he left the bathroom. I climbed
down off the toilet seat, my knees so weak I could
barely walk and my chest heaving in convulsive gasps
as I tried to breathe again. But, I was very, very quiet.
I did not whimper, cry, or make a sound as I went to
my room and got into my bed.

The next thing I remember is waking during the
night because my legs were stuck to the sheet. Some of
the welts on my legs had cuts in them. The cuts had
bled, and the blood had dried as I lay sleeping. When
I jerked my legs loose, the cuts opened and bled again.

A Vocabulary Lesson

That "spanking" was only one of many. Sometimes I was told to lie face down on my bed. Other times I had to stand on the toilet seat. Always the blows were to the backs of my legs. And always the blows would stop only when I stopped crying.

These beatings—for that is what they really were—often were followed by outpourings of affection from my father. He would hug me tight and tell me how very much he loved me. He told me he spanked me because he loved me.

And I believed him. The connection between love and pain was made early.

My father referred to himself as "strict," and seemed to pride himself on "spanking" his children when they deserved it. His use of these words created in me a distorted view of discipline as well as the absolute conviction that I was a very bad little girl indeed since I seemed to need spanking so often.

Ever the journalist and amateur pollster, I remember asking other children throughout my childhood if their fathers were strict and if their fathers spanked them. Nearly everyone I asked nodded solemnly and said that, yes, their daddies were strict. Many children said they had been spanked, but usually added that it was only if they had been very bad.

I never pressed them further to see if their definitions of these terms were the same as mine. I just assumed they were. Many years would pass before I would learn that my spankings were not spankings; they were beatings. And that my father was not strict, but sadistic.

At the time, though, I concluded that what my father did to me was what all daddies did when children were bad. Since I seemed to get it much more often than anyone else I knew, however, I decided that I must be very, very bad.

Tommy, Can You Hear Me?

My brother Tommy was nearly five years younger than me. He was incredibly bright and funny and active but, we agreed, he must have been a very bad child, too, for he received many beatings at our father's hands. I never knew what his beatings were for, and I never saw them because all of these beatings (mine and my brother's) took place behind closed doors. I only heard my brother's terrified, anguished cries until he, too, somehow willed himself to be quiet so the hurting would stop.

After a beating, my brother and I were ordered to stay in our rooms with the doors shut. We were not allowed to speak to one another. I remember desperately wanting to comfort my sobbing little brother and hating my father for separating us.

Once we lived in a house where my brother's room and mine shared a wall. The wall had a heating vent near the floor. We often lay on the floor and talked to each other through the vent, using pillows to muffle our voices. We said things like, "Shhh. It's O.K. now," "You'll be all right," "I love you," "I hate him," and "I'll never hurt my kids like that." This communication was such a small victory, but it gave us comfort and courage.

More Lessons

While our father did not yell or scream when he was beating my brother or me, he was given to fits of rage at other times, usually over small irritations and sometimes for no reason we or our mother could discern. These rages were fearsome and dangerous; his cursing and insults went on for hours. We tried to take refuge in our rooms, but he would draw us out to verbally batter us some more.

My brother and I often commented after these terrible scenes that we wished he had "just hit" us because, unbelievable as it sounds, the insults our father hurled at us and the disgust, even hatred, in his eyes when he looked into our own were far worse, far more painful in every sense than any beating we ever received. When I look back on those days, I can no longer feel the sting of my father's belt on my legs, his hand taking my arm in a bruising grip, or his fingers pinching my neck until my knees buckled and my vision blurred, but I can call to mind so easily the despair and hopelessness I felt in my father's presence. I knew, even as a small child, what it felt like to have your heart break.

Since that time, I have known other hardships and experienced many losses, but it was during those years with my father that I learned the most painful lessons of my life. I learned that, no matter how good I was or how hard I tried at anything, I would never please my father. I learned that, if something or someone hurt me, it was my own fault. And, I remember the most wrenching grief imaginable as I grew through those awful years and came into the realization that, no matter what my childish expectations and romantic notions of life and love might have been, they were dead wrong. Whether I liked it or not, love hurt, and I had just better get used to it.

A Compassionate Observer

Domestic violence experts often speak of the *compassionate observer* or *helping witness*, a loving adult who enters into the life of an abused child from time to time. This witness repairs a little of the damage to the child's self-esteem and provides a sense of hope just by his or her caring presence and obvious delight in the child. Sometimes the compassionate observer is not aware of the good he is doing and may not even realize the child is living in an abusive home.

I am prayerfully grateful for the times I was able to spend with my grandfather, a quiet man who worked most of his life for the railroad in a small Texas town. I spent many happy summers at my grandfather's home. We fished in the lake, went into town for the mail and the newspaper, bounced thirty miles in a pickup truck to buy barbecue, made peach ice cream, and spit watermelon seeds. He thought I was wonderful and told me so. I am convinced those times, brief though they were, and my very special compassionate observer planted in me a small seed of confidence that would not bear fruit for many years to come, but which, when I grew sufficiently desperate about my life, blossomed forth and saved it. I would be thirty years old before I would awaken from a lifelong nightmare, empowered by a righteous anger, and begin to unlearn those terrible lessons my father taught me.

Mom

Readers who have not personally experienced domestic violence will be asking by now, "So where was your mother when these beatings took place?" Those who have been there will understand.

First of all, it is important to know the context of these events. They began in the mid-1950s and ended in the late 1960s. Domestic violence and child abuse didn't exist in most people's minds during those years except in the most severe cases that made occasional news headlines, cases where abandoned children were discovered feasting on garbage or a parent was accused of murdering a child. Whatever happened within the framework of the family was considered to be a very private matter, and outsiders did not interfere in private matters. Neighbors did not call the police when they heard screams from next door. Teachers did not ask about welts on children's legs. And, wives and mothers certainly did not discuss these matters outside the home. The father was head of the household in most families, but in a violent household, no one— including and maybe even especially the mother—challenged the father. Ever. About anything.

My father did not beat my mother. However, if she argued with him or cried, he twisted her arm behind her back until she was quiet. For her, too, the hurting only stopped when she grew silent.

The techniques of control he used more often with my mother included humiliation and insults, hostility, threats of suicide (his own father had committed suicide when my father was a teen-ager), and open infidelity.

As will be discussed in greater detail in a later chapter, abuse is always about power and control. My father was in complete and utter control of everyone in his house including my mother. She spent her life with him walking on eggshells, trying to make everything perfect, constantly exhorting my brother and me to remember to avoid all the behaviors or comments that might make our father "go off," always reminding us not to cry.

Divorcee was an ugly word in the fifties and sixties. The connotations were many for my mother, a "nice girl" from a conservative Southern Baptist upbringing. A divorcee was seen as a failure, a woman who had not been able to keep her husband happy. Due to some flaw in her character, it was assumed, she had been a disappointment to him and he had left her. And, of course, there were the inevitable rumors that plagued divorcees of that day. They were viewed as loose women and became social outcasts. Because they were considered morally questionable, they certainly weren't welcome at gatherings where other women's husbands might fall under their spells. No way would my mother have become a divorcee during those "Leave it to Beaver" days, the "Ozzie and Harriet" years, the era of "Father Knows Best."

Above all, my mother was a victim of abuse just as my brother and I were. Leaving an abusive husband has never been an easy thing to do; in the 1950s and 1960s—with no battered women's shelters, no domestic violence hotlines, no support of any kind for victims of domestic violence, leaving was virtually unheard of.

So, my mother did what we all do when we believe we have no way out. We keep a stiff upper lip, and we survive from one day to the next. We make ourselves believe things are not as bad as they sometimes seem. Just as I learned to stop breathing and make my mind go blank in order to survive, so my mother learned the survival skill of concentrating on the good times and pretending the bad times didn't happen or at least weren't really all that bad.

The Beginning of the End

As my brother and I grew older, the beatings became fewer, but our father's reign of terror continued. His violent outbursts of insults, screaming, and cursing became almost daily events, and each was more terrifying than the last. At other times, he was cruelly sarcastic; he enjoyed telling my brother and me to "dummy up." Nothing we did pleased him. Our grades were never good enough. I did not display either talent or enthusiasm for the music our father loved so much. My brother had not turned out to be the athlete our father had wished for. Our mother's "faults" were so many that he actually made a written list of them for her reference.

My father seemed to be especially angered by my transition from little girl to teen-ager. He turned away from me in disgust when he saw that I had been experimenting with make-up and trendy clothes or when he heard me talking with my girlfriends about boys. He called me "boy-crazy" when I was thirteen; by the time I was seventeen, I was a "slut," even though I had never engaged in anything more than a goodnight kiss at the end of a date.

Just as we all remember where we were and what we were doing during moments of personal as well as public crisis, I remember clearly the night I stopped trying, the night I stopped caring, the night I became resigned to the fact that there was nothing I could do to forge the relationship with my father for which I had always longed. I told myself that night that it was the last time he would ever hurt me, that the tears I cried that night were the last I would ever shed because of him. One might expect that such a turning point would have occurred following a particularly violent episode, but it happened quickly and quietly.

It was during a family dinner one evening. I brought up a question about the war in Vietnam. My high school civics teacher had raised the question that day and told us to find out how the members of our families felt about the issue. As a prelude to posing the question, I told my mother, father, and brother that gathering their opinions was part of my homework assignment.

My father laid his fork down, put both hands in his lap and glared at me. "Do you have a Ph.D.?" he asked me.

"No, sir."

"And does your civics teacher have a Ph.D.?"

"No, sir."

"Well, I do. You can tell your civics teacher that I will discuss world affairs with you when you have a Ph.D. And I will share my opinions with her when she has one."

We finished that dinner in silence just as most dinners in our house were eaten. I remember looking down at my plate the whole time, my eyes stinging with tears of embarrassment, hurt, and anger.

In spite of my intentions that night, I have cried enough tears over my father to float a battleship since that sad, silent family dinner twenty-five years ago. But, the difference between the tears I shed when I lived with him and the tears I have shed since is that the latter have been of the healing sort. Just as a nasty wound must be drained, cleaned, and disinfected if it is to heal, so, too, must our emotional injuries be opened up and treated. We do that by sharing our hurts with loved ones or friends who know how to listen without judging, seeking professional guidance when necessary, and praying for wellness and wholeness.

Out of the Frying Pan

The awful years of living in the same house with my father ended when I was seventeen and my brother was twelve. Our father came home one afternoon, ordered us all into the living room and announced he was leaving us. I don't remember much of what he said. My mother sat stunned and silent. I didn't move or speak, but my heart was dancing and I was thinking *at last!*

What I remember most clearly is that Tommy, his voice a little shaky, but his stance courageous, said, "You mean it? You're leaving?"

When my father said yes, he was really leaving, my brother said, "Good. Now I can tell you how I feel about you. I hate you. You always said you loved us, but you only hurt us. I'm glad you're leaving. Don't you ever come back here and hurt us again."

I was so proud of Tommy that day. He had said what was in my heart, too. There was nothing my father could say. He had relinquished all authority and control. He gave us one final disgusted look and left. My brother shut the door behind him.

. . . And into the Fire

Our abuser had left. But, as so many abused women and children know, we often look for someone to replace the abuser. Not consciously, of course. No one ever says, "Whew, I'm glad I'm rid of that man who beat me! Think I'll go find a new man to beat me."

Unless we have a deep awareness of what is wrong in our lives and what is right, an understanding of where we have been and where we want to go, and confidence in our perceptions, judgments, and decisions, we are drawn to what feels familiar. I had no awareness, no understanding, and precious little confidence. I was drawn to a young man who felt familiar.

Adam Holt (not his real name) was nineteen when we met. I was seventeen. He was movie-star handsome and slightly dangerous in a rebel-without-a-cause sort of way. I was a bookworm, always a little nervous, almost always lonely. Adam worked in the shipyard during the week, drank and partied on the weekends. I was a senior in high school who made decent grades and took part in speech and drama activities. He thought I was cute, and he was surprised and pleased to learn I was a virgin who didn't drink or use drugs or otherwise carry on like so many of our sixties contemporaries. In his presence, I felt like a good girl, very feminine and protected by his badness. For the first time in my life, a man (other than my grandfather who had passed away) whose opinion mattered to me praised me for being a "good girl" and was impressed by my virtue.

We had our first argument on one of our first dates. Adam was angry because I had told him I knew how to get to a party we were going to at a friend's house, but we got lost and had to call and get directions. He demanded to know why I had told him I knew where we were going when, apparently, I did not. I didn't have an answer, which only made him angrier. His anger felt familiar. I felt like a bad girl who had behaved stupidly. I bought into his assertion that the evening was ruined and it was my fault. My humiliation and sadness felt familiar, too. He left me alone in the yard for awhile to think about what I had done.

Later, he came and found me sitting in the grass. He smiled and told me all was forgiven. I walked six inches off the ground the rest of the evening.

Thus began a stormy relationship that would last thirteen years. When I look back on those days now, I find it very sad that I allowed someone as manipulative and emotionally abusive as Adam to become the center of my world. I want to take every young girl who has been abused by her father and say, "Please listen to me! Learn from my mistakes and the mistakes of millions of women before you! Let us tell you what your life will be like if you don't face the abuse you have suffered right now so that you can ensure you are never a victim again. Run—don't walk!—as fast as you can away from any man who feels familiarly like Daddy."

The signs that our relationship would be disastrous were there from the beginning, but I was very young, very lonely, and very abused. Too immature to look for more substantive qualities, I was impressed by Adam's good looks, his charm, and humor. When he was two hours late picking me up for a date, when he flirted with other girls everywhere we went, when he took off with his friends for days at a time, I believed it was my fault. I just had to improve myself, make myself more attractive, more fun to be with, more charming, more interesting. If I got my feelings hurt, my heart broken, I had no one to blame but myself. Adam said so, and my past bore it out.

With Adam, as with my father, though, it was just so hard to figure out what the rules were, and it became increasingly difficult as the years went by. The rules changed all the time. Sometimes, when I thought I had done something that would please Adam, he either didn't notice at all or was displeased. A cake I spent an entire day baking and decorating for him received not even a passing comment. A new color of eye shadow or lipstick brought only an irritated "Go wash your face."

Always there were rumors about other girls. He usually denied them, but sometimes admitted he had spent time with another girl; there was always an innocent explanation. Inevitably, he tied his conduct to something specific I had said or done or neglected to say or do. My faults were many in his eyes, and he told me about them endlessly. Everything he did to me that hurt me was justified, he said, by my own behavior. This made perfect sense to me. After all, it was how I had been raised.

This pattern would continue throughout the years we dated and the nine years we were married. Hindsight tells me I was a very desperate young woman. I had never dated much before I met Adam and was convinced no one else would have me. He reinforced this belief with regularity.

As twisted as it seems to me now, when my boyfriend was angry with me and hurting me, I felt at home. That's not to say it was comfortable or that I even thought I was happy. I knew I was miserable most of the time, but that misery felt familiar and I felt responsible for it. Besides, I asked myself, what was the point in dwelling on it? In my experience, this was how relationships between men and women played out. It was just how they were. I tried not to think about how unhappy I was. Instead, I spent all my time trying to be prettier, smarter, wittier, more fun, more stylish—whatever Adam's requirement of the week was.

Marriage and a Family

We became engaged when I was twenty-one. I remember being a bit muddled and confused, thinking I should be the happiest I had ever been. Why did I feel so empty and numb? Why was I in such a hurry to marry this man? Immaturity and past experience made me believe Adam was the only man who would have me and that, once married, I could make him so happy he would stop hurting me. Somewhere in the back of my mind, though, a little voice was telling me it would only get worse. I have very few regrets in my life, but one of them is that I did not listen to that little voice. Except for the enormous blessings of my two sons, nothing good would come from what I was about to do.

We married a year later. The first bitter fight came only a few months into the marriage. He had gone out of town for several days with some friends to an athletic event. I raced home from my teaching job the day of his return to make a special dinner and plan a romantic reunion. He had told me he expected to be home by four or five o'clock. The hours ticked by and I grew increasingly worried until finally, around nine o'clock, I called his parents.

He was at their house. He had been there all afternoon and evening watching television with his father and brother. I was angry, but Adam was angrier. When he came home, he shouted at me that I had embarrassed him in front of his parents by "tracking him down" and that I was never to track him down again, that he would come home when and if he felt like it. He threw some of my clothes into an overnight bag and, after punching a hole in the bedroom door, pushed me out the front door of our apartment.

I stayed in a small motel for several days. He found me, told me he was sorry our argument had gotten out of hand, but it was my fault to begin with for embarrassing him in front of his parents by calling him there. He waved his hand in the air as if to make it all go away and said, "Come on. Let's forget it. Pack up your stuff and come home." Of course, I did.

During the nine years we were married, he physically pushed me out of our home three times, but the second and third time I did not leave. I just sat outside until he let me back in the house.

Power and Control

Adam seemed to take pleasure in hurting my feelings in subtle ways I now recognize as control techniques. He often said things like, "This new girl at the office makes all her own clothes and even makes handbags and headbands to match every outfit. She is so stunning," and "So-and-so doesn't wear make-up like you do. She is naturally beautiful, and that natural look is so sexy," and "You are so pale. Why don't you get a tan like so-and-so?"

When I did something that pleased him, Adam literally patted me on the head or shoulder and said, "Good girl!" This happened when he found his shirts all hung facing the same direction but not touching one another, the spice rack arranged in alphabetical order, and the laundry hamper, washer, and dryer empty simultaneously.

Most of the time, I was not allowed to have money; if Adam did give me money, I had to be able to account for every penny and there had better not be any purchases of which he had not approved ahead of time. In spite of the fact that we both had good jobs, there was never any extra money according to Adam. I had to give him my paycheck at the end of each month. He kept the checkbook and gave me checks when I needed to go to the grocery store or to shop for something specific or when it was time to sit down and pay the bills. When I went out of the house with a check, I had to bring him the receipt for whatever I bought so that, when the canceled checks came back, he could see that I had not written the check for more than the amount of purchase. I never saw his paychecks.

Sometimes my mother paid for the children's prescriptions when they were sick so that I wouldn't have to ask Adam for the money. He became very angry any time one of the boys or I went to the doctor. Explaining "well baby check-ups" to him was next to impossible. Any kind of illness represented weakness to Adam. He regarded with contempt people who got sick, and he himself was never sick during all the years I knew him. Go figure.

We almost never socialized in any way with other couples. Adam said there wasn't enough money. I was not allowed to bring up the fact that he went out with his male friends four or five nights a week and on frequent out-of-town trips with them to attend athletic events. He frequently alluded with a grin to "the ole double standard," which, to his way of thinking, justified pretty much anything that a man wanted to do.

Holidays were among the worst times. The house always had to be immaculate, but Adam became particularly obsessed with neatness and order during the holidays. As gifts were unwrapped, paper and ribbons had to be neatly folded or put into the trash immediately. One item at a time. Very organized. Afterward, everything had to be cleaned up, spit and polish. The whole house had to be vacuumed, and this by midmorning of Christmas Day. Chores that were usually spaced out over several days or a week all had to be done on Christmas Day.

Adam always considered our house to be his. I was allowed minimal decorating input (I could choose the curtains, but I couldn't hang pictures on the walls), but I was not allowed any input into other decisions about the house, such as what color the living room would be painted or where the new patio would be poured; I often came home from work to find that such major changes had been made to our home while I was gone, and I knew better than to complain. I was not allowed to use the closet in our bedroom, but had to use the one in the hallway. I was not allowed to use the bathroom in the master bedroom suite; mine was the bathroom down the hall. I was not allowed to sleep late on weekends. Adam said Saturdays and Sundays were work days just like any other, the only difference being that I had a different job. He checked my vacuuming by leaving bits of paper under the bed and behind doors. I was not allowed to turn on the air conditioner unless the humidity plus the temperature added up to a number he had predetermined (it changed from year to year). I had to ask his permission to turn on the heat in the winter; the answer was often, "No. Go put on a sweater if you're cold." We had a beautiful fireplace in the den, but I was not allowed to use it. Adam said it was too messy, the same reason he gave for our seldom using our outdoor grill.

Insults and Threats

Adam had always been short on patience, but after the boys were born, he had none. Everything they did infuriated him, from their crying and spitting up as infants to their curiosity and mischievousness as toddlers. My faults multiplied tenfold. Now, Adam reminded me daily, I was "fat," "damaged goods," "ugly," "stupid," "emotionally disturbed," and (most painful to me) "a lousy mother."

He knew that, before the boys were born, my greatest fear was of abandonment and the loss of (what I mistook for) his love. He played on this fear with comments like, "For every pound you gain, that's another pair of my socks in the suitcase" and (when I was pregnant) "Sleeping with you is like sleeping with a beached whale." He always laughed when he made these remarks; he thought they were funny and said that my problem was I couldn't take a joke. It seems ironic to me now that the more this abusive man criticized and insulted me, the more desperate I became to hold onto him. Such is the nature of abuse.

After the boys were born, my greatest fear became the loss of them, and Adam knew how to play on that fear, too. When I began to bring up the subject of divorce, he told me in no uncertain terms that, because of his training in the credit and finance industry, he knew how to disappear without a trace and that he would not hesitate to take the boys and do just that. Once, while watching a television movie about a man who kidnapped his two children after his wife filed for divorce, Adam said, "I swear to you I would do that." When the mother in the movie experienced anguish over the loss of her children, Adam said she had brought it on herself. When she succeeded in getting them back, he pointed out the mistakes the father in the movie had made. Adam said that if he took our boys, I would never see them again. I tried harder and harder to be the perfect wife, mother, housekeeper, and teacher so that Adam would not leave me and would not take my children from me. But, the harder I tried to knit our little family together, the faster it unraveled.

In the Interest of Fairness

In one surprisingly generous move, Adam took me shopping for dining room furniture after he had won a large sum of money in a tournament. He said that the trophy meant more to him than the cash, and that he knew how much I wanted to furnish the dining room.

It is only fair to say that acts such as this, while extremely rare, did occur when Adam was in an especially good mood. More important to me, however, were the small acts of kindness and affection which he sometimes displayed. There were many of them during the early years of our marriage, sandwiched though they were between eruptions of violence. As the years wore on, those small acts became fewer and fewer, and they grew further and further apart, but the occasional sweet smile or wink could still make me forget the bad times and believe things were going to turn around. After our first child was born, Adam even said, "I have fallen in love with you all over again," and he was very sweet and attentive for a while. The romance didn't last long, however, and by the time our second child was born less than two years later, Adam was "too busy" to even bring us home from the hospital.

I had yet to learn the important lesson that abusive people are not abusive all the time, that most of them are not abusive to anyone except their partners and children, and that they are often witty, charming, enchanting, and popular people with everyone except their victims. As far as I knew, Adam was well-liked by everyone who knew him, both socially and through his work. This only served to reinforce my belief that I was somehow to blame for my misery.

Escalating Violence

During the last months of our marriage, Adam's abuse became more physical. When angry, he shoved me up against a wall and shouted in my face. Sometimes, he poked me with an index finger on my chest just above my breasts. On a few occasions, he pushed me to the floor. These violent acts were accompanied by his enraged shouting, name-calling, and insults.

Sometimes he threw or kicked things at me. The objects I remember most vividly were a green plastic trash can from the bathroom that he kicked the length of the hall hard enough that it split open and nearly hit our older son (who was just beginning to crawl) in the head, and the sneakers he tore from our younger son's feet and threw against the wall next to me, missing my head by a few inches.

All of these scenes were followed within a few days by Adam's apology that things got out of hand, but the apology always contained a reminder that it had been something I had done or not done that had made him angry to begin with.

One of the worst fights occurred after a Sunday visit from Adam's parents. I moved the high chair from its usual corner to the kitchen table so the baby could sit with his grandparents and Adam and me while we adults had coffee. When I moved it, a dust ball whooshed into the middle of the room from where the high chair had stood. Adam's face went stony. My heart sank. I knew what that look meant.

The fight began after his parents left and was the only one that ever left a mark on my body. The next morning, I had some small bruises on my neck and chest from Adam's poking me with his finger. I covered them with make-up and went to school. Midway through the morning, a young man appeared at my classroom door with a dozen long-stemmed red roses for me. Adam had sent them, but the note bore only his name, nothing more. I remember how confused I was when my colleagues told me how lucky I was to have a husband who sent me flowers at work! I remember thinking over and over again during that day and throughout those confusing years, "What on earth is wrong with me?"

An Evening Out

One of the very few social events we ever attended (near the end of our marriage) was a sports awards banquet. I was introduced to several people that evening who said they had known Adam for years, but had no idea he was married.

Around 11:30, I told Adam we needed to leave. We had told the baby-sitter we would be home by midnight. The baby had been sick with an ear infection, and I knew he would be waking up soon; he would need medicine and to be fed. Adam became irritated and said very firmly that he was not ready to leave. Two young women who seemed to be friends with Adam said they were going to continue the party at their apartment and asked us to drop by. I told them we really had to go home.

Adam was silent as we left the building. By the time we got to the parking lot, he had his hand around my upper arm in a viselike grip. He shoved me toward the car, got in, and drove like the proverbial maniac, shouting at me all the way home. "I can't have any fun anymore! You don't know how to have fun! Everything is babies with you!" He pulled up in front of the house, reached across me and opened the car door, pushed me out onto the curb, and drove away. He stayed out all night.

The Day the Love Died

I began leaving Adam shortly after our first child was born. I say "began leaving" because leaving is seldom a one-time thing. Most women leave their abusers an average of three to six times; some leave many times more than that before they finally escape. I left three or four times. I'm not sure how many because some of our separations were more official than others, and one or two were very brief. Each time I left, I got a little stronger, a little braver, a little more determined to change the course of my life. Each time I came back, I became a little surer that I needed to get out for good.

It was somewhere between two of these separations that whatever was left of the love I had felt for Adam withered and died. Ironically, as with my father, it didn't happen during a violent episode, but when words were said that did more damage than any push or shove ever had.

I had won a poetry contest sponsored by the local newspaper. Adam had read the poem the night before I submitted it, and he had pronounced it "stupid." I was so excited when I learned I had won that I called Adam at work to tell him. I blurted out the good news, then waited to hear what he would say. There was only silence. After long seconds, I said, "Well, what do you think?" He said, "I think somebody else liked your *stupid* poem."

Pearl Bailey once said, "Sometimes I would almost rather have people take away years of my life than take away a moment." Adam had taken my moment.

Getting Strong

Adam stayed away all night more and more often. In hindsight, I think we both knew our marriage was over, but he had always said he would never divorce me. He loved the term *injured party*, and always said that, if we ever divorced, he would make sure everyone knew he was the injured party. He often said that, if he decided he wanted out of the marriage, he would make me so miserable that I would have no choice but to divorce him.

He finally did it. The last straw was the night he came home in the early hours of the morning and I asked him where he'd been. The question so infuriated him that he pulled me from the bed and began shoving me around the room while shouting at me that whatever he had been doing, wherever he had been, and whoever he had been with were none of my business.

I was yelling, too. I had had enough and was finally standing up for myself and my children. I shouted at him that it most certainly was my business because

I was his wife, that he had a home and a family who needed him, and he had better start coming home to us.

He looked surprised, but recovered quickly. He accused me of "going toe-to-toe" with him "like a man," and said if I wanted to fight like a man, he would treat me like one. He used a bed pillow to push me around the room, then began swinging it like a baseball bat and hitting the sides of my head with it. Finally, he threw me on the bed, sat on top of me, and pushed the pillow down over my face.

Suddenly I heard, "Daddy, stop hitting my mommy! Daddy, please stop! Daddy, don't!"

Adam jumped off the bed, snatched up our older son who was standing in the bedroom doorway, took him back to his own room, and threw him onto his bed. I heard my child hit the wall. Before I could get across the hall to him, Adam was on his way out the front door.

I ran to my son. He wasn't physically injured, but he was hysterical. Both of my ears throbbed and burned from having been hit with the pillow. I knew the trauma of this night would remain with both of us for a long time.

My son grew quiet and a little calmer after a bit of rocking and reassuring talk. I then took him and the baby (who had slept in his own room through the whole incident) into my bed where they quickly fell asleep. I locked all the doors, checked all the windows, and then shut the bedroom door and put a chair under the knob like I had seen done in the movies.

I sat on the floor beside the bed for the rest of that night with the telephone and a kitchen knife by my side. If Adam had come back in the house that night, I would have called the police. If he had hurt my child again, I believe I would have killed him or died trying.

I spent the night thinking about my current situation within the context of my whole life. As a child, I had promised myself that I would never hurt my kids like I had been hurt. It hadn't occurred to me then that someone else might hurt them. I decided that night that I would not allow it. We were getting out. I wasn't afraid of being alone anymore. Even if I spent the rest of my life without a partner, I realized, it would be better than this.

Getting Out

I saw an attorney the very next day and began the process of filing for divorce. The attorney warned me not to leave the residence because Adam could charge me with desertion which could improve his chances of gaining custody of the boys. He also informed me there was no way to force Adam to leave since both our names were on the deed to the property. He basically told me there was nothing I could do but wait for the papers to be served on Adam and pray he would leave on his own.

Adam at first acted delighted that I had taken the first step. He boasted that he had been seeing someone else for some time, and that it really was best for us to just part company and begin our lives again. He moved out of the house on Halloween. I thought the timing very appropriate, sort of as if the house had been exorcised of its demons.

But, as is so often true in cases of domestic violence, things went from bad to worse during the next months. I had a locksmith change the locks. Adam pounded on the front door many nights, vowing to make my life a living hell if I didn't call off the divorce. I called the police on those nights. They came, told him to leave, then left when he did. He came back each time, more furious than before. I called the police again. I felt they were more exasperated with *me* each time, and I finally quit calling them.

Other nights, Adam called on the phone. He cried and said he had never believed I would really leave him, that if I would just call everything off, he would change and we would be happy. Each time I said no, that this time was final, and asked him to please leave me alone. That only sent him into a rage again.

Many of Adam's behaviors would today be considered stalking. He said he had a friend of his who lived in the neighborhood watching me all the time and reporting back to him. Adam left notes under my car's windshield wiper to let me know he knew where I went, what I did, and who I saw. Sometimes he called just to shout and curse at me. If I hung up, he called back. Again and again and again. He was relentless. If I took the phone off the hook, I could expect him at the front door within half an hour. Sometimes he just sat in his car in front of the house.

Adam's behavior was becoming more and more irrational and obsessive. He was scaring me more than at any time during our marriage.

Frustrated and frightened, and on the recommendations of friends and relatives, I hired another attorney. Knowing absolutely nothing about the judicial system, we were all certain that if I could just get in front of a judge and tell my story, he would help me. The new attorney told me that Virginia is a no-fault divorce state. She said that, since I had no eyewitnesses (other than the children) to any abuse and no photographs of injuries or physician's records describing injuries, the best and perhaps only way to get a divorce from my abusive husband in the state of Virginia in 1982 was to tell the court—via paperwork, of course—that it was no one's fault. I recall feeling utter disbelief, helplessness, and hopelessness. How could all that my children and I had endured be no one's fault?

Adam was radiant with triumph when he learned that ours was to be a no-fault divorce. He took that to mean that his treatment of us was just fine and dandy with everyone but me. His interpretation was that even the law said everything he had done was okay.

Free at Last

The divorce went forward, slowly but surely, and I found that, in spite of the almost constant threats and harassment, I was beginning to enjoy my newfound freedom. For nine years, I hadn't slept late, fixed what I wanted to eat for a meal or a snack, hung a picture on a wall, picked a paint color or a wallpaper, used any bathroom I wanted to, or hung my clothes in my own closet. My enjoyment of these and other simple pleasures which so many people take for granted grew into delight and wonder over the next months, and finally became part of the peace and contentment I now experience every day.

The years since I declared my independence from abuse have not been easy by any stretch of the imagination. Battles with my ex-husband alternately raged and waned for years. My father's overwhelming disappointment in and disapproval of me have arrived from time to time by way of letters in the mail. I have faced countless minor frustrations and numerous serious problems in raising two headstrong sons who witnessed domestic violence in their early years. And, I watched my brother die far too young at the age of thirty-three.

But, there has been more good than bad. I found new love with a warm and gentle man who made it his mission in life to show me that love doesn't hurt and love is consistent. I found renewed joy in watching my beautiful sons grow and learn. I found new commitment to creating my own happiness, new energy for living each day, and new faith in myself and in God. Like the soldier in the poem at the beginning of this chapter, I have grown a wing where I lost an arm.

You can grow wings, too.

I am not afraid of storms for I am learning how to sail my ship.
—Louisa May Alcott

I have been driven to my knees many times
by the realization that I had nowhere else to go.
—Abraham Lincoln

And then a hero comes along
With the strength to carry on
And you cast your fears aside
And you know you can survive
So when you feel like hope is gone
Look inside you and be strong
And you'll finally see the truth
That a hero lies in you.

—from "Hero"
by Mariah Carey

I have always grown from my problems and challenges,
from the things that don't work out. That's when I've really learned.
—Carol Burnett

Chapter Three

Why You Must Help Yourself

Too Little, Too Late

One of the most frustrating aspects of working in the field of domestic violence prevention and intervention is the difficulty of identifying the victims and providing them with available services before it's too late. All too often, the caring and knowledgeable individuals who provide shelter for battered women and children shake their heads over their morning newspapers as they read yet another account of a life lost in a battle that raged in a home just down the street or across town. "If we had only known," they say as they comfort one another. "If we had only gotten to her in time."

The case of Nicole Brown Simpson is just one of many thousands of such tragedies, but it illustrates in a dramatic way how so many other scenarios play out. Married to former super-athlete and handsome movie star O.J. Simpson, Nicole had tried to conceal for years the fact that her husband abused her both emotionally and physically. Friends and family members knew, though. She also had been treated in a hospital emergency room and had called 911 for emergency assistance on numerous occasions. O.J. had even been convicted of spousal abuse.

Then, just after midnight on 13 June 1994, Nicole's mutilated body and that of her friend Ron Goldman were discovered on the walkway in front of her elegant Los Angeles condominium. As this is being written, O.J. Simpson sits in a California courtroom where he is on trial for the brutal killings. It appears at this time that it would take a stunning evidentiary blow to the prosecution's case, a startling confession by someone else, or a jury with an agenda of its own that has nothing whatever to do with justice for the defendant to go free. But, considering everything else that went wrong from the very first time O.J. Simpson acted less than lovingly to Nicole, it will surprise few if this man slips through yet another crack in the system. Stranger things have happened in our justice system.

According to an article in *People* magazine (20 February 1995), which detailed Nicole's relationship with O.J., red flags should have gone up all around Nicole when she returned from her first date with O.J. seventeen years before her death with her jeans ripped. She told a friend that O.J. had torn them in his eagerness to "make love."

Throughout their years together, family and friends now report having witnessed O.J. embarrass and humiliate Nicole in public many times, and they report having seen bruises on her face and arms. Many who knew the couple and some who just lived in their neighborhood heard the former star running back threaten his wife and shout obscenities at her.

Denise Brown, Nicole's sister, testified in court that she was present when O.J. "threw (Nicole) against a wall, picked her up, threw her out of the house" during an argument. Following another abusive incident, Nicole asked Denise to take pictures of her injuries and later locked the photos in a bank box for safekeeping. The two women's father was even shown the photographs.

Denise also cited incidents in which Simpson made crude jokes about parts of Nicole's body when the two were in public together, even grabbing her private parts and making loud, lewd comments. Nicole was mortified.

Ron Shipp, a family friend and police officer *with special training in the area of domestic violence*, did try to talk to O.J. after a particularly violent episode during which the police were called, but later intervened on O.J.'s behalf by pleading the case to one of his superiors.

That episode occurred on 1 January 1989. Two police officers responding to an emergency call from Simpson's North Rockingham home were met by a bruised and shaken Nicole who cried, "He's going to kill me. He's going to kill me. You never do anything about him," as she clung to one of the officers. O.J. reportedly commented to officers, "You've been out here eight times before, and now you're going to arrest me for *this*? This is a family matter. Why do you have to make a big deal of it?"

O.J. was charged with assault and pleaded no contest. Judge Ronald R. Schoenberg ordered Simpson to make a $500 donation to a shelter for battered women, to pay a $470 fine, and to undergo domestic violence counseling. The counseling he received was minimal at best, and when O.J. later moved to the East Coast on an NBC assignment, he was permitted to continue his counseling by telephone. Some reports have indicated that O.J. Simpson took part in only three or four counseling sessions, one or two in person, one or two by phone. Who knows? No one was paying much attention.

The police were called to both the Rockingham address and to a condominium to which Nicole moved when she and Simpson separated, but no official reports of further assaults have been found.

While it is known that Nicole was treated at least once in a hospital emergency room for injuries inflicted upon her by O.J., it is not known whether the attending physician reported his suspicion of abuse to anyone who could have reached out to Nicole. He did tell investigators later, however, that he had not believed her story of having fallen off her bike.

Nicole Brown Simpson finally reached out to the people who might have helped save her life only five days before her death. She called and requested advice from Sojourn Services, a battered women's shelter near her home. Whatever the good people at the shelter told Nicole, it apparently convinced her she could put a stop to the violence in her life. She is reported to have told friends a few days later that her life was taking a turn for the better and that she was excited about the future. She promised to tell them all about it soon, but they never saw her again. Nicole Brown Simpson took her plans, her hopes, and her dreams with her to her grave.

Some Hard Truths

Seventeen years of abuse. Not every day, not every week or month. Maybe many months went by during which O.J. behaved lovingly toward the woman he claimed to adore. Certainly, there are at least as many witnesses to his acts of kindness and affection toward Nicole and others as there are witnesses to his violence, but therein lie some of the most important and yet hardest to accept truths about spousal abuse: If your partner has hurt you *even once*, he is abusive and you are a victim of domestic violence. If he has hurt you *even once*, he will do it again. And, if he has hurt you *even once*, the next time will be worse. He may be Mr. Nice Guy 90 percent of the time and a terrifying, abusive bully only 10 percent of the time, but the longer you remain with him, the more the balance of those percentages will shift, and the greater will become the risk to you and your children of serious injury or death.

As we are all learning from this horrible story that is still unfolding, friends, family, neighbors, doctors, the police, and the judicial system all had the opportunity to intervene at some point to help Nicole, but no one did. Why? The answers to that question will help you understand that, while there are many systems in place that can protect and support you, you must first help yourself.

Relatively Speaking

Victims of domestic violence cannot rely on family members to point the way for them or come to their rescue. This doesn't mean their relatives don't love them or care about the fact that abuse is taking place (although, sadly, sometimes this is the case). It only means that family members often fail to recognize the violence taking place in the home of a daughter, sister, cousin, or other relative, and they seldom offer any constructive assistance even when they do recognize it. They fail to respond for a number of reasons.

First of all, they may really and truly never see or hear any evidence that any abuse is taking place. I would only be tempted to believe this is the case if the family members are widely separated geographically (say, by an ocean or most of Asia) and seldom or never communicate with the victim. Still, it could happen.

Other reasons are far more likely. One is that a large percentage of abusers are incredibly charming, congenial people who are never abusive or violent to anyone except their spouses or in the presence of anyone but their spouses. So, while relatives may have seen occasional evidence of abuse (a little bruise on the arm, a red mark on her cheek) or the victim may have reported to them that she is being abused, they find it hard to believe that anything more than a lovers' quarrel has occurred. Since an abuser isn't abusive twenty-four hours a day, seven days a week, year in and year out, the victim's family members are among the easiest people to fool unless they live in the same home with both the abuser and victim, or unless they are especially observant and trust their instincts.

Even when family members begin to notice signs that a relative is being abused, it is extremely hard for them to admit it because, once admitted, part-ownership of the problem and responsibility for helping to find a solution become inevitable next steps. Ownership and responsibility in such a serious matter as abuse can be frightening and can often mean major life changes such as the victim and her children moving in with family members or requesting financial assistance from them. Many family members, sad to say, don't want a relative's problems affecting their own lives. They may be heard to say things like "I've got troubles of my own," "She's a grown woman. She can take care of herself," and "If it gets bad enough, she'll leave."

Others refuse to admit a loved one is being abused because they feel it somehow reflects on them. Surprisingly, some parents of victims do not see that a daughter is being abused because they subconsciously fear what her victimization may say about the way they raised her. They may worry about what the neighbors might think or say about them. The victim's father may have been abusive himself and believe that, if his daughter's husband is beating her, she must deserve it. The victim's mother may herself have been a victim of abuse and so may see her daughter's situation as normal. In most cases, family members with a history of domestic violence will have no trouble blaming the victim, even if she is their own daughter. If there was no violence in the family in which the victim grew up, her parents may be so thoroughly puzzled by what they see happening to their daughter that they simply enter into a pattern of denial (denial is explained in further detail in chapter 4).

Family members in denial will encourage the victim to "kiss and make up" with her abuser. Other dangerous comments victims often hear from relatives include "There are two sides to every story," "Stand by your man," "It's up to the woman to keep the family together," "Running away from the problem doesn't solve it," and "You must have done something pretty awful to make him that mad!"

At the other extreme are family members who become so enraged when they learn of a relative's victimization that they become part of the problem by instigating violence themselves. They may go storming into the victim's home and begin a physical altercation with her abuser. They may call him on the phone and threaten him. None of their hostility accomplishes anything, of course, but to escalate the violence immediately and further endanger the victim and everyone else involved.

Family members may also become judgmental. The victim may have left her abuser several times and moved in with relatives. After they have seen her thus come from and go back to the abuser a few times, they may lose patience. "If it's so bad," they ask her, "why do you keep going back to him?" Judgmental remarks only further isolate the victim from her family and make her less likely to confide in them again or turn to them when she is in danger.

These are just some of the reasons family members cannot be relied upon to protect and advise victims of domestic violence. These are the reasons why, historically, families have not provided reliable guidance.

Of course, that doesn't mean these reasons are acceptable. Families absolutely must become involved and find out what they can do to help a member who is being abused. Families absolutely must become the first line of defense for victims. Some ways of doing that are discussed in the last chapter of this book.

Friends

Like family members, friends often fail to recognize that someone they care about is being battered. Because they may never see what most people consider evidence of abuse (black eyes, bruises, broken bones, etc.) or see it only occasionally, they find it easy to assume that the friend and her partner are no different from other couples who quarrel every now and then. It's easy to think, "So they had an argument that got a little out-of-hand. I'm sure it won't happen again."

It's even easier to think, "I'm her friend, but this really isn't any of my business." Getting involved is scary and involves some emotional risks (and possibly even some physical risks in the worst cases); thus friends may detach themselves from the intensity of the situation by ending conversations that turn serious and becoming less accessible. Because battered women are often depressed and nervous and sometimes hysterical and frantic, they are not always comfortable people to be around, so their friends may abandon them. Once again, the victim's isolation increases. Just when she needs family and friends the most, they turn away. It's not because they don't care; it's because they don't understand. It's because they are frightened. It's because they don't know what to do.

That doesn't make it OK. It's not OK to turn away from a friend who is in any kind of trouble, especially trouble that puts her life in danger, but it is understandable. Again, the last chapter of this book spells out specific ways in which friends of battered women can help.

The Emergency Room and
Your Family Doctor

Considering the facts that 22 percent to 35 percent of the women who seek medical care in hospital emergency rooms are treated for injuries resulting from domestic violence and that medical expenses from domestic violence total at least thirty-five billion dollars annually, you might think that doctors and emergency room personnel would be thoroughly educated and trained to recognize the signs of domestic violence. You might assume they would spring into action to first treat the victim and then counsel her. You might believe they would report their suspicions to authorities. In most cases, you would be wrong.

While some states now require medical personnel to notify authorities when they suspect spousal abuse, hundreds of thousands of domestic violence-related injuries to women are never mentioned outside the treatment room. In many cases, the causes of the injuries are not even discussed *in* the treatment room!

In one astounding case, a woman sought help in an emergency room for knife wounds to her head, face, and neck. The cuts required a total of twenty-seven stitches to close. The attending physician never asked the patient how she received the injuries!

Dr. Gail Bundow, an emergency room physician in a hospital in the South, is a former victim of spousal abuse who says that, in all the times she was treated for injuries inflicted by her husband, not once did a physician ask her how she received those injuries. In the June 1994 issue of *Redbook*, she told reporter Jan Collins Stucker of her years as a battered wife and the frustration she experiences today with many of her colleagues in the medical profession.

"As a result of domestic violence," Dr. Bundow told Stucker, "we are seeing millions of women in our emergency rooms and in our doctors' offices. But we're just putting on Band-Aids. We're not fixing the problem."

She cites an unwillingness to become involved, fear of offending the husband, and time constraints as some of the reasons doctors don't question patients and intervene when they suspect abuse. She also suggested that maybe they'd just rather not know.

"They might play golf with the woman's husband. It's easier just to give the woman medical care."

Once again, this response is not acceptable, but it is real and it is true and it happens every day in medical centers throughout the country and the world. Until every state requires physicians and other medical personnel to report suspected cases of spousal abuse and until those professionals conscientiously involve themselves in every suspected case of domestic violence, you must help yourself.

The Police

The most chilling political cartoon I have ever seen was one that appeared on 1 July 1994. Artist Don Wright of the *Palm Beach Post* cut right to the heart of the problem of police involvement in violent domestic situations. The illustration depicts a woman lying on the ground in a semifetal position, her shoes missing, her dress a twisted mess, her hair across her face, and a pool of dark liquid near her head. The police officer standing calmly over her and writing in his notebook asks, "Did you provoke him?"

Yes, the situation really is that bad. "The National Crime Victimization Survey Report," based on interviews with approximately four hundred thousand individuals, states that police officers are "more likely to respond within five minutes if the offender (is) a stranger than if the offender (is) known to the female victim." As that report and Wright's cartoon suggest, police officers often fail to take domestic disputes seriously and/or they often blame the victim.

Law enforcement officials around the country really began to take domestic violence seriously and to accept greater responsibility for protecting the victims after Tracy Thurmond won a $2.6 million lawsuit against the police department of Torrington, Connecticut, in 1984. Thurmond had repeatedly called the police for help when her husband threatened and abused her, and she was brutally attacked by him—beaten, kicked, and stabbed with a knife—in the presence of their young child. According to some accounts, a Torrington police officer witnessed part of the attack but did nothing to stop it, nothing to protect the victim, and nothing to subdue her attacker. The vicious assault left Thurmond partially paralyzed and with other permanent physical disabilities. She was able to prove that the department had failed to protect her from her abusive husband.

The problem in most cases is not a genuine lack of compassion on the part of the police, but a lack of competent and comprehensive training in the complex and dangerous area of domestic violence. It is hard to be understanding when you really don't understand what's going on, and a large percentage of officers really don't understand the dynamics of domestic violence.

Historically, police officers—who should be a victim's fastest and most reliable help when she is in danger—have not been especially tuned in to the dynamics of family violence. They have chastised victims for their hysterical tears and disorientation, they have asked victims why they are still there and haven't left their abusers, they have asked victims what they did to make their abusers angry, they have advised victims and abusers to kiss and make up, and worst of all, they have left victims and abusers together at scenes of domestic violence after seeing that everyone involved seems to have calmed down. Too many times, this has left the victim even more vulnerable to renewed attack by her abuser.

When challenged regarding their responses to domestic calls, some officers are fond of saying that they are not social workers or therapists. That's fine. No one expects them to be. However, we do expect them to protect and serve and to save lives whenever possible. In order to protect victims of domestic violence and ultimately save lives, it is absolutely crucial that every police and sheriff's department in this country provide in-depth and ongoing training on this subject and that every employee of these departments— from secretarial staffs to dispatchers to beat-cops to police chiefs and commissioners—be required to participate in such training.

I recently spent a day at a regional police training facility to observe a training session on domestic violence. (The training session was scheduled for eight hours, but actually lasted a little less than six after subtracting the lunch hour and numerous breaks. *Less than six hours* in which to learn about a subject as complex as domestic violence!) I had looked forward to learning valuable information from the presenters, speakers, and instructors. However, I learned much more that day from listening to the comments made by the law enforcement students in the classroom. Here are a few examples:

- "I hate these touchy-feely things." (This was said following a female presenter's request for students to introduce themselves.)
- "My first wife was an abusive bitch, so I shook her and got a new one."
- "She would only do it once!" (This was said in response to a female presenter's statement that

a victim of domestic violence may turn her anger and frustration on the officer.)

- "She caused it." (This was said following a description of a violent domestic call and in reference to the victim.)

And, one of the instructors actually made the following remarks:

"I love to fight. I'm a very aggressive officer."

"People shouldn't hit on each other, but thank God they do or we wouldn't have jobs."

The atmosphere exhibited by many of the male students throughout the day in that classroom was one of machismo, aggressive posturing, especially when the presenters were female. The student who made the comment about his first wife repeatedly waved his hand during a presentation by a young woman who counsels victims at a battered women's shelter. When she called on him, thinking he had a question, he pointed to his watch and loudly informed her that the class was overdue for a break. He was rude and domineering. His entire manner suggested that no woman was going to exert any control of any kind over him, even if it meant holding him up for five minutes when he wanted to be doing something else. I pity and pray for the victims of spousal abuse to whose calls he will someday respond.

During an exercise called a *practical* in which the instructor asked four students to do some role-playing to demonstrate how to diffuse a violent domestic situation, the two students who were asked to assume the roles of homosexual lovers appeared embarrassed and upset and started to return to their seats while shaking their heads no. Finally, they reluctantly agreed to do the exercise when the instructor told them it was necessary to understand and be prepared for calls involving same-sex relationships. A lot of snickering went around the room and some ugly remarks were made.

I could only think about one of serial killer Jeffrey Dahmer's last victims, a teen-age boy whom police found naked and bleeding on the street. Believing the boy to be older and the victim of a gay lovers' quarrel, the officers took the boy back to Dahmer and handed him over to the demented man who would later torture, murder, and dismember him. After handing the victim over to Dahmer, the officers laughed and made the same kind of crude jokes I heard at the police academy that day.

Certainly, no one can dictate or control how another person feels or what he thinks about the lifestyle of another human being, but when an individual chooses a career in law enforcement, it is imperative that he or she be emotionally mature enough to put aside personal opinions and never allow those opinions to interfere with the safety of another person. If he is not able to do that, he has no business wearing a badge.

On the other hand, I saw signs of hope in that room that day. There were many young men in the classroom who exhibited genuine concern and a desire to know more. They admitted not understanding why victims return to their abusers time and time again, and they admitted their frustration with domestic "call backs" (addresses to which they have responded many times for the same types of problems) and with victims who don't press charges or bring charges only to drop them the next day. But, the dynamics of family violence can be taught and learned, and these students expressed a willingness to learn and a desire to understand and help. They will make fine police officers.

There also were eight or nine female students who appeared to be quite capable of taking care of themselves in the presence of their male classmates. They ignored and refused to be baited by sexist remarks and put-downs. One young lady held her head high as she stated her goal of being chief of police one day and didn't react or respond at all when the male students laughed at and made fun of her. Another mentioned that she had experienced violence in her own life. These female students were more attentive to the instructors and presenters and generally more involved in the learning process than many of their male classmates. They, too, will make fine police officers.

I was especially gratified to learn that the son of the executive director of a shelter for battered women was among the students in the class. I believe it can be safely assumed that he has special insight and sensitivity to the plight of battered women and that he will be an asset to his department and his community when he hits the streets.

The instructor even surprised me when, after having made those earlier macho remarks, he ended the class saying, "Caress these calls. When taking a victim's statement, treat her like she's your mother or your sister. If her abuser has limited her relationships, you may be the first person she has ever been able to talk to about the abuse. Be gentle."

It is essential for victims of domestic violence to know that, if and when they choose to call for police assistance, they may be met with officers who are less than sensitive to their situation, less than knowledgeable about domestic violence, and less than caring about women in general. And, yes, there are police officers who beat their wives. Yet another reason why you must help yourself.

The Legal System

For the victims of domestic violence who choose to report their abusers, police officers are often the first point of contact with the legal system. Depending on the responding officer's level of training in domestic violence and personal commitment to helping victims of abuse, that initial contact can be the beginning of a woman's successful escape or it can increase her isolation, further convince her that her victimization is her own fault, and send her reeling back into the battering arms of her abuser.

One of the saddest truths about domestic violence is that the same is often true of the other professionals a victim may meet along the way of the confusing, intimidating, and sometimes cruel legal process. Every day, countless women give up hope of ever escaping the violence in their lives because they have met with ignorance and prejudice in the courthouse. Many victims come away from courthouse meetings and courtroom procedures saying, "I feel like I've been beaten up again."

For all their degrees, for all their training, and for all their promotions up the ladder—some all the way to the bench—many lawyers and courthouse officials view domestic violence as nothing more than the inability of a man and woman to get along. They believe both to be equally to blame for their problems, and they routinely tell couples to learn to get along with each other.

Often, unless there are x-rays of broken bones or photographs of blackened eyes and open cuts, judges rule that no abuse occurred. Some do not want to hear testimony about abusive incidents. Some refuse to listen at all; some appear to listen, but they don't really hear what the victims are saying to them. Some are intolerant of a victim's tears. These are the officials who routinely fail to take the decisive actions that would protect the victims and punish the abusers. These are the officials who put the abusers back on the streets to hunt their prey again. It is as if they are deaf and blind to the facts that a crime has taken place and there is a perpetrator of that crime and a victim.

During the final weeks of preparing the manuscript of this book, yet another woman died at the hands of her abusive boyfriend in the community where I live. Tamekia Daniels was shot and killed by James Bailey less than three months after he was charged with malicious wounding for stabbing her in the shoulder, a charge for which he was ordered held on a five thousand dollar bond. Twenty-four hours later, a judge reduced the bond to one thousand dollars. Bailey paid the required 10 percent of the bond—a mere one hundred dollars—and was released. Bailey continued to terrorize Daniels and threatened to kill her, resulting in a summons to appear in court two months from the date of the summons. He killed her before he had to appear in court. Four days later, he shot himself in the head. Does that mean that particular cycle of violence, the Daniels-Bailey cycle, is ended? Absolutely not. Tamekia left a four-year-old son behind.

I was sickened when, a few days later, I read that the Chicago Bulls had been fined twenty-five thousand dollars because Michael Jordan wore the wrong jersey number in a game. The team and Jordan were warned that they would be fined an additional twenty-five thousand dollars and would face further discipline for each future game in which Jordan wears the wrong jersey number, adding up to a possible total fine of approximately six hundred thousand dollars by the end of the season plus that "further discipline." Michael Jordan and his team were punished more severely for violating a uniform rule than James Bailey was for stabbing Tamekia Daniels. Maybe we should consider turning wife beaters and child abusers over to the NBA. At least they take it seriously when people break the rules. Our legal system could take a lesson.

A recent broadcast of "60 Minutes" told the story of Betsy McCandless-Murray, a forty-two-year-old systems engineer. McCandless-Murray sought help from the courts after leaving her husband Sean Murray. She had left Murray after repeated beatings which left her with a broken nose and cracked ribs, among other injuries. The court did issue a restraining order which ordered Murray to stay away from her and not contact her in any way, but Murray violated the order repeatedly. When Betsy reported the violations to the court clerk, she was met with indifference according to family members and friends. Five months after leaving her husband, Betsy was shot and killed by Murray, who then shot and killed himself.

The same broadcast told the story of Donna Bianchi. Donna's husband was released on bail and granted visitation rights with his children after being charged with attempting to murder his wife! Less than twenty-four hours after he was granted visitation with their son, Robert Bianchi murdered Donna by shooting her five times. Another story told of Judy Dickenson's fears that she will suffer the same fate as Betsy and Donna because the judge in her case has given her abusive ex-husband joint custody of their children. In cases such as these, the courts have not only given tacit approval of the abuse, but also have provided the abusers with plenty of opportunity and access to their victims.

Of course, there are many fine people working within the legal system, and with time and attrition, I believe they will infuse that system with more realistic legislation, stronger enforcement, and greater humanity. They have their work cut out for them, however. An article entitled "He's Going to Kill Me" in the September 1994 issue of *Glamour* magazine reported, "The joke in the (Albuquerque) courthouse is that some prosecutors operate on a 'fifteen-minute rule.' Translation: If they themselves want to batter the woman after fifteen minutes of talking to her, then they either reduce the charges or don't pursue the case at all."

That pretty much sums up the attitude millions of women have encountered in the legal system.

The following letter to the editor appeared in the *Daily Press* (Newport News, VA) on 28 March 1995:

> I am a victim of domestic violence. My life, and that of my son, has been irrevocably changed.
>
> We had to flee from our home for fear of our safety and hide from my abuser for fear of retaliation. I have been bruised and battered and have had broken bones, but those are the wounds that will heal. The invisible wounds of humiliation, the loss of my dignity and the psychological abuse will remain for a lifetime.
>
> Through the support and encouragement of my family and friends, I mustered up the courage to get out of the abusive situation and take action against my abuser. I was confident that justice would be served, and my day in court finally arrived.
>
> Little did I realize that my personal tragedy would be met by the cold indifference of the legal system. Obviously, there was a history of physical and verbal abuse that led up to the final act of violence, but that was not admissible in court. As a matter of fact, my attorney was informed that 'the court didn't have all day' and he needed to speed things up. So within less than 30 minutes the court, in its infinite wisdom, found the abusive attack not to be 'an intentional act.' . . . The court did not really seem to take the matter seriously at all. . . .
>
> The horror of abuse in any form is a killer. It robs humanity of pride, confidence and self-worth. The courts refuse to make the abuser accountable for his actions, so he does not receive the necessary help he needs to stop the

abuse. *In the end, the court system has made victims
of us all* [emphasis mine].

The Good News

I don't want to end this chapter without emphasiz-
ing the abundance of good news and good people in
the field of domestic violence. Many women's lives and
the lives of their children have been saved by observant family members and friends who insisted on learning the truth and, once discovered, refused to minimize it. Those family members and friends contacted
the shelters and organizations qualified to counsel the
victims and help them make decisions; and those family members and friends stood by the victims throughout their ordeals. God bless 'em.

Likewise, many lives have been saved by competent and compassionate police officers, family physicians and emergency room personnel, private attorneys, city prosecutors, and judges.

Progress is being made in all these areas. The
American Medical Association's new guidelines on
domestic violence state that physicians "should routinely inquire about abuse as part of the medical history," and that they "have an obligation to familiarize
themselves with protocols for diagnosing and treating
domestic violence and with community resources for
battered women and their children." Much more is
needed, especially in terms of requiring medical personnel to report suspected cases of abuse, but this is a
start.

Many major cities now have domestic violence
teams, groups of professionals with different areas of
specialization who work together to help victims escape the violence. A program in Phoenix teams police
officers with mental health professionals and trained
volunteers who respond together to domestic violence
calls. Albuquerque (in spite of the lack of compassion

of some members of its district attorney's staff) has a highly specialized unit called DART (Domestic Abuse Response Team). According to the *Glamour* article cited earlier, this city is one of the first in the country to have developed a specialized police unit specifically devoted to the problem of domestic violence. DART members are trained in the interviewing of victims, understanding the psychology of abusers, making charges stick, and getting abusers into court.

The San Diego Police Department has one of the most comprehensive and advanced training programs in the country, a program designed and implemented by Sgt. Anne O'Dell. One of the many valuable tools used in San Diego is a letter which is sent to a victim following a reported incident of domestic violence. The letter is from the chief of police and informs the victim of support services available to her and of personnel standing by to assist her, as well as telephone numbers and other information to get the victim headed toward help if she so chooses.

Sergeant O'Dell has developed an instructional program called STOP DV (Specialized Training On Preventing Domestic Violence) and travels extensively to bring this program to police officers and other professionals that they might better meet the needs of victims of domestic violence. If more police departments and municipal court systems took advantage of such training and other resources available for the asking from jurisdictions around the country which have experienced success in dealing with domestic violence, we could go a long way toward protecting victims from further abuse.

There is more good news in the Violent Crime Control and Law Enforcement Act which was signed into law by President Clinton on 13 September 1994. This document contains the long awaited and much needed Violence Against Women Act, which, according

to the January/February 1995 issue of the newsletter
Update published by the National Coalition Against Domestic Violence,

> mandates interstate enforcement of protective or-
> ders, establishes a National Domestic Violence
> Hotline, provides training for state and federal
> judges, enables victims of gender-motivated
> crimes to sue their attackers in federal court for
> violating their civil rights, and begins to ad-
> dress the needs of undocumented women who
> are abused by their husbands.

The newsletter further states,

> One million dollars has been appropriated to
> establish the National Domestic Violence
> Hotline.... Additional federal money for shel-
> ters, youth and community programs to address
> sexual assault, domestic violence and child abuse
> will not be appropriated until FY '96. At that
> time, battered women's shelters will receive an
> appropriation of $50 million under the Family
> Violence Prevention and Services Act with $10
> million increases in each of the following two
> years.

And, yet, more good news exists in the form of a
recent program brief published by the U.S. Department of Justice's Bureau of Justice Assistance. The brief
is entitled "Family Violence: Interventions for the Justice System," and it provides a listing of "critical program elements needed to intervene effectively in family violence." Its authors refer to these program elements as "ambitious," and indeed they are, but they
represent nothing more than elements which have been
needed all along. The identified elements include early
case identification and response, coordination among
designated personnel, written policies, a "vigorous and
affirmative" prosecution effort, formal entry of court

orders, formal monitoring and enforcement, specialized training for personnel, and strong leadership from
judges, prosecutors, public defenders and others within
the legal system. The fact that this brief exists in writing today underscores the fact that the system has
been without these critical elements to date, but it also
is evidence that somebody somewhere is paying attention at long last. Maybe something will come of it.

What All of This Means for You

Very simply, unless you are extraordinarily lucky,
no one is going to rescue you from the violence in
which you live. You must come to terms with the abuse,
make the decision to leave, and then get out. The
following chapters will tell you how to do that, but only
you can turn information into action. You must be
your own hero.

God is our refuge and strength, a very present help in trouble.
                                                    —Psalm 46:1

*One cannot get through life without pain. . . . What we can do
is choose how to use the pain life presents to us.*
                                                    —Bernie S. Siegel, M.D.

It's Okay
by Laine Parsons

*It's okay to be afraid
of the thing we don't understand.
It's okay to feel anxious
when things aren't working our way.
It's okay to feel lonely . . .
even when you're with other people.
It's okay to feel unfulfilled
because you know something is missing
(even if you're not sure what it is).
It's okay to think and worry and cry.*

*It's okay to do
whatever you have to do, but
just remember, too . . .
that eventually you're going to
adjust to the changes life brings your way,
and you'll realize that
it's okay to love again and laugh again,
and it's okay to get to the point where
the life you live
is full and satisfying and good to you . . .
and it will be that way
because you made it that way.*

Chapter Four

Admitting You Are Abused

Could I Really Be a Battered Woman?

Throughout the first seven or eight years of my first marriage, I never once thought of myself as abused or battered. I knew those terms, of course, but thought they only applied to women whose jaws had been shattered or whose eyes had been blackened, or who had suffered some other serious physical injury at the hands of their husbands or boyfriends.

I remember wondering to myself, *So what is it when your husband is just plain mean to you, when he shouts at you all the time and pushes you around, when he calls you names and blames everything that goes wrong on you? What do they call it when he plays mind games and stays out half the night every night, when he tells you it's none of your business where he's been, when he insults you, when he just plain acts like he can't stand the sight of you?*

I usually shrugged off the questions with the assumption that it's not called anything because it isn't anything at all, that it's just the way marriage is.

Sometimes I tried to talk to a friend about what my life was like, how lonely and depressed I was, how scared I was of my husband's "temper" (that's the strongest word I ever used for it back then). She said, "You really need to sit down and talk to Adam," implying that talking to him would solve everything. I just nodded my head in silent agreement, feeling hopeless, too embarrassed to explain that I couldn't talk to Adam, and knowing, even if I did try to explain, my friend wouldn't understand. No one seemed to understand, so I stopped trying to explain and figured that, just as Adam said, it was all my fault.

I couldn't talk to Adam because, when I tried to explain how I felt, he told me I was "crazy," emotionally disturbed, "weird." When I told him I wanted him to come home nights and spend some time with the children and me, he called it "browbeating" and "badgering."

When the violence escalated near the end of our marriage, I still didn't think of myself as abused. I only realized that Adam's temper seemed to be getting worse all the time. It took less and less to set him off. It might be that one of the babies was crying or had spit up on the furniture. It might be his rushing into the house with only twenty minutes to spare before meeting his friends for a night out and his dinner not being ready. It might be my asking for money for a doctor's bill arriving in the mail. Anything and everything, little things and nonexistent things—there simply was no way to predict what might drive him into a rage the next time. Once again, as I had for so many years in my father's house, I walked on eggshells.

I didn't make my decision to leave until that eye-opening evening when I saw the effect of what was happening on our children and realized the situation had moved dangerously close to someone getting seriously injured. Still, I did not think in terms of abuse.

Looking back on the woman I was then, I realize that I went through my days just going through the motions zombielike, making myself numb most of the time so I could get through the day, terrified when Adam was home, nervous when I thought he might be on his way home. Toward the end, I didn't even cry anymore. I felt dead inside.

I left the marriage with two little ones in tow and never looked back. In a way, my "hardening of the attitude" was a blessing. This time I didn't listen to Adam's pleas and promises. This time I didn't melt when the romantic cards came in the mail, when the flowers were delivered to my classroom, when the children came home from weekend visitations with gifts for me from their father.

I left the marriage because I saw the violence escalating. I answered the wake-up call and left when I knew someone was going to get badly hurt, maybe even killed. I left when I realized that, even if I spent the rest of my life alone, it would be a better life than the one I had.

That is the message I want you to begin repeating to yourself. It is the message I believe saved my life in more ways than one. Tell yourself again and again, "Even if I spend the rest of my life alone, it will be a better life than the one I have now." Now say it again. And again. And again.

It will be a better life than the one you have now because it will be free of violence and abuse.

And you know, whether you have admitted it yet or not, that nothing could be better than that.

Denial: Friend or Foe?

Denial is the powerful psychological force that causes us to deny that a situation is as bad as it is. The first response of many people to the news of a sudden death is, "No, it can't be true!" The wife whose husband is having an affair may look the other way and pretend not to know what is going on. The grown children who see their parents' mental and physical health begin to decline may act as if nothing is wrong.

We enter denial when reality is too painful to look in the eye. We enter denial when we believe that, if we look at a situation directly and admit that it is terribly serious, we will be faced with decisions we think we are incapable of making. We enter denial as a way of protecting ourselves from what we believe will be unbearable.

Counselor Jack Tallman of Tustin, California, explained the five stages of denial in an interview with the *Orange County Register*. His descriptions of these stages and my examples may help you determine whether you are in denial of your own abuse.

Stage one is denial and isolation. The battered wife may say, "I can't believe this is happening to me."

In the second stage, there is depression coupled with regret and hindsight. The battered wife may say, "If only I had made French toast instead of pancakes."

In stage three, a person finally accepts responsibility for the dynamics of the situation. She says, "It's time to make a change." By the way, accepting responsibility does *not* mean you are responsible for the violence or abuse. It means you are responsible for deciding what you are going to do about it.

Stage four is marked by appropriate anger at the right person for the right reasons. The battered wife accepts the experience of abuse and begins to plan how she will change her life.

Stage five is acceptance with action. The battered wife deals with the unfair pain, frees herself of the denial, and leaves the relationship.

Does any of this sound familiar? Do you see yourself somewhere in stage one, two, or three? Just for a few minutes, admit that it's possible you have been denying the fact that you are in (or have been in) an abusive relationship. Don't berate yourself. You haven't done anything wrong. Maybe you have been denying because everyone else, including and maybe especially your abuser, tells you that you're not being abused. Maybe they've told you and you've told yourself that it's not abuse unless you've had a black eye or a broken arm. Maybe you have been denying because, even though you *have* had a black eye or a broken arm, it "only happened once and he didn't mean it." Maybe you have been denying because you are afraid of what your abuser will do to you if you stop denying and start getting out. Whatever the reason, if you have been in denial, it was your mind and spirit's way of protecting you at the time. It wasn't a good thing or a bad thing; it was simply self-defense.

But, now it's time to stop denying and start getting out.

Defining the Abuse

Okay, you say, you're willing to consider the possibility that you are in an abusive relationship and that you have been in denial until now. But, of course, you want to know for sure before you go any further with this.

When so much conflicting information comes at us from our parents, siblings, boyfriends or husbands, friends, co-workers, doctors, and lawyers, how are we supposed to know if the reason we feel so bad all the time and live in fear is that we are being abused?

We answer a few questions, that's how. And, we answer them honestly and without fear of what the answers mean because no one ever has to know the answers but ourselves if we so choose.

Verbal and Emotional Abuse

The National Coalition Against Domestic Violence offers the following questions as indicators of verbal and emotional abuse.

How many of these things has your partner done to you?

- ignored your feelings
- ridiculed or insulted women as a group

- ridiculed or insulted your most valued beliefs—religion, race, heritage, or class
- withheld approval, appreciation, or affection
  as punishment
- continually criticized you, called you names,
  shouted at you
- humiliated you in public or in private
- refused to socialize with you
- kept you from working, controlled your
  money, made all decisions
- refused to work or share money
- took car keys or money away from you
- regularly threatened to leave you or told you
  to leave
- harassed you about affairs he imagined you
  were having
- manipulated you with lies and contradictions
- threatened to hurt you or your family
- abused, tortured, killed pets to hurt you
- destroyed furniture, punched holes in walls,
  broken appliances
- wielded a gun in a threatening way

The NCADV publication which lists these questions goes on to acknowledge that many of us do some
of these things when we are in a bad mood (although
I would caution you to be aware that many of these
behaviors—and especially the last four—are serious
indications that you and your children may be in immediate danger). So when are they classified as abusive?

Ask yourself some more questions, advises the
NCADV. Do you doubt your judgment or wonder if
you are "crazy"? Are you often afraid of your partner
and do you express opinions less and less freely? Have
you developed fears of other people and tend to see
others less and less often? Do you spend a lot of time
watching for your partner's bad and not-so-bad moods

before bringing up a subject? Do you ask your partner's permission to spend money, take classes, or socialize with friends? Do you have fears of doing the wrong thing or of getting in trouble? Have you lost confidence in your abilities, become increasingly depressed, and feel trapped and powerless? If you answered "yes" to many of these questions, it is probable you have been abused and have changed as a result of being abused.

In her book *The Verbally Abusive Relationship* (Holbrook: Bob Adams, Inc. [1992], 73), Patricia Evans says that "verbal abuse constitutes psychological violence" and that "all domestic violence begins with verbal abuse." If you are in a verbally abusive relationship, you are living in violence and you are an abused woman.

Physical Abuse

The beginning of physical abuse is often verbal abuse that escalates to threats of physical violence. When your partner says things like "I'll punch your lights out" and "I'll break your neck," he is taking the step across the line that separates verbal abuse from physical abuse. Sometimes, abusers don't make threats; they just cross the line and go right from verbally abusing their victims to physically abusing them. Once your abuser has crossed that line and/or done any of the following to you, you are a victim of physical abuse:

- held you to keep you from leaving or blocked your exit
- shoved, pushed, hit, slapped, punched, choked, kicked, or bit you
- thrown or kicked something at you
- locked you out of the house
- driven recklessly with you in the car
- forced you off the road or kept you from driving

- abandoned you in a dangerous or secluded place
- refused to help you when you were sick, hurt, or pregnant
- raped you
- threatened or hurt you with a weapon

Sexual Abuse

Sexual abuse is common in relationships ranging from couples on a first date to couples who have been married to one another for many years. Many young women are unaware that sexual demands or unwanted and uncomfortable touching from a date are abusive, and so many people still believe in the concept of "wifely duties" that married women are often sexually abused without realizing it. You have been sexually abused if your partner has done any of the following to you:

- forced you to have sex or to perform sexual acts with which you are not comfortable
- called you sexually derogatory names (such as "frigid") and criticized you sexually
- hurt you during sex
- publicly showed sexual interest in other women or otherwise humiliated you sexually
- had sex with other women after committing to a monogamous relationship
- forced you to have sex when you were frightened, ill, hurt, or when having sex was a known danger to your health

The following information is from the newsletter *Thoughts from Turningpoint* (Spring, 1991):

Marital rape is defined as any type of sexual activity that is forced or coerced from a wife who is unwilling to perform it. It is not an infrequent problem. An estimated two million incidents occur annually. Women who are sexually assaulted by their husbands many times do not define the incident as sexual assault. Since the assault occurred within the context of marriage, they may believe that their husbands have "sexual rights" with or without their consent.

The following is a list of women's rights regarding marital rape:

1. Every woman has the right to make decisions about having sex, using birth control, and becoming pregnant. She does not lose these rights if she marries.

2. No one, including her husband, ever has the right to force a woman to have sex, either through physical violence or through threats of harm to her, her children, or another person.

3. A woman does not become the "property" of a husband when she marries.

4. If a woman and her husband have disagreements about sex, they should try to resolve their differences through talking or by seeing a counselor.

5. If a husband rapes his wife, it has nothing to do with whether or not they have been having sex. It is an act of anger designed to degrade, humiliate, and punish the wife.

Victims need to learn to view marital rape as sexual assault for which they are not responsible. They should not remain silent victims.

Abuse Can Be Insidious . . . or Almost Instantaneous

Another important characteristic of abuse is that it is often insidious, occurring gradually over a long period of time. The frequency and the intensity of the incidents increase over time. What may have been in the second year of marriage a nasty insult becomes by the fifth year a little push or shove and by the seventh year of marriage a punch or a kick. It doesn't have to happen all at once in one horrendous incident to be abuse. Domestic violence can be so insidious that the victim doesn't realize what is happening to her. Often, many years go by before the situation becomes extremely dangerous and she finds herself asking, "How did I get here?"

On the other hand, some abusive relationships escalate very quickly. Many women have died at the hands of abusive men they have known only a short time. That is why it is so important to know the warning signs which you will find later in this chapter.

Why Does He Do It?

Partner abuse is always about *power and control*. The abuser's intent is to establish power over his victim so that he can control her behavior. Each time his treatment of her achieves the desired result, he receives the message that what he did to achieve the result is okay. After all, it worked. Therefore, he reasons, it will be okay to do it the next time she is "out of line." And, if she begins to argue or refuses to cooperate, he reasons that it will be okay to step up the level of violence until he again gets the result he is looking for.

In their book *Intimate Violence* (New York: Simon and Schuster [1988], 22), Richard Gelles and Murray Straus offer the "social exchange theory" in answering the question "Why do men hit their partners?" This theory, say the authors, "assumes that human interaction is guided by the pursuit of rewards and the avoidance of punishments and costs."

Gelles and Straus illustrate the theory by pointing out that, while an abuser might hit his wife because the house isn't clean, he would not be likely to hit the cleaning lady if the house wasn't clean. And, while an abuser might hit his own child for breaking something, he would not be likely to hit a visiting child who broke something.

Why would these abusers not hit the nonfamily members? Because effective social controls exist to prevent that kind of assault. A man who hit the cleaning lady or a visiting child would be subject to criminal charges and penalties (if convicted) which might include fines and/or jail time. Therefore, the reason he doesn't do it is because he can't get away with it and he knows it.

The simple answer, then, to the question "Why do men hit their partners?" is "because they can." They do it because, historically, they have not suffered any consequences for their battering behavior. In other words, they have always gotten away with it. They do it because no one intervenes to stop them. They do it because no one punishes them for doing it. And, they do it because it gets them what they want, i.e., it works, even if only until the next time.

The Cycle of Violence

Women who are in abusive relationships routinely experience what experts call the "cycle of violence." The cycle consists of three phases. The first is a period of tension building during which the victim bends over backwards ("walks on eggshells") to try to keep the inevitable explosion from happening. Then, there is the violent incident which occurs in spite of everything the victim has done to try to avoid it. The violence is followed by a "honeymoon" period during which the abuser tries to make up for his violent acts and seems remorseful. This cycle repeats itself over and over and over again, generally escalating in severity. The length of time from the beginning of the cycle to the end generally becomes shorter and shorter.

Do People Ask You "Why Do You Stay?" Tell Them . . .

"Why do you stay?" is not a valid question to ask of a battered woman. Staying in an abusive relationship is not a crime. Battering another human being is. If someone asks you, "Why do you stay?" remind them of this, then tell them to ask instead, "Why do men hit?"

I'm not going to belabor this issue because, again, it's not a valid question when asked by others, but you may find yourself getting down on yourself for staying and wondering why it's so hard for you to admit you are abused and to make the decision to get out. So we'll look at it, but only briefly.

Why do we stay?

We stay for many different reasons. We stay because we fear retaliation, because we feel guilty, and because we have been brainwashed into believing we are worthless. We stay because we are afraid of being alone, we are afraid of losing custody of the children, and we are afraid of being homeless and hungry. We stay because we love him, and we stay because we don't know how to leave him. And, we stay because we get accustomed to the abuse.

One of the best explanations I have ever heard for why we stay in abusive relationships is a story cited by Patricia Evans in her book *The Verbally Abusive Relationship*. The story tells of a scientist who wanted to see at what temperature a frog would abandon water. She put the frog in a tray of cool water. The frog stayed. She gradually warmed the water. The frog stayed. She made the water hotter and hotter and hotter. Still the frog stayed. The frog remained in the tray of water until it boiled to death.

The reason is acclimation. The frog adapted so gradually to its increasingly hostile and dangerous environment that it couldn't save itself although the way was wide open.

Acclimation is self-defense.

Who made the water hot?

Enough said.

The Warning Signs

The following list of behaviors seen in people who are abusive was compiled by Sandy Meadow of the Women's Center at Old Dominion University in 1992. Ms. Meadow based her list on information drawn from a number of experts including Lenore Walker, Ginny NiCarthy, Scott Lindquist, the Duluth (Minnesota) Program Development, the National Coalition Against Domestic Violence, and the Project for Victims of Family Violence.

> Below is a list of behaviors that are seen in people who are abusive. The last five signs listed are almost always seen only if the person is a batterer; if a person has several of the other behaviors (three or more) there is a strong potential for physical violence. The more signs the person has, the more likely the person is a batterer. In some cases, a batterer may have only a couple of behaviors that the woman can recognize, but they are very exaggerated (extreme jealousy over ridiculous things, for example). Initially the batterer will try to explain his behavior as signs of love or concern, and a woman may be flattered at first. As time goes on, the behaviors become more severe and serve to dominate the woman.
>
> 1. Boundaries. Violates your personal space. Intimidates you by getting too close. Touches, pinches, grabs you against your will.
>
> 2. Quick involvement. Sweeps you off your feet. Love at first sight. "You're the only one for

me." Desperately pressures you for a commitment so you're engaged or living together in
less than 6 months.

3. Controlling behavior. Controls where you go,
what you do, with whom and for how long.
Controls money and money decisions; won't
allow you to share expenses or refuses to work
and won't share expenses. Protective to the point
of controlling. Says he's angry you're late because he cares. Takes your car keys; won't let
you go to church, work or school. *You got we need to seperate*

4. Jealousy. Angry about your relationships with
other men, women, even children and family.
This insecurity and possessiveness causes him
to accuse you of flirting and having affairs, to
call frequently or drop by to check up on you,
even check your car mileage or have you followed.

5. Abusive family of origin. Was physically, sexually, or emotionally abused as a child or witnessed spousal abuse. He sees violence as normal behavior, a natural part of family life.

6. Low self-esteem. Guards his fragile sense of
self by acting tough and macho. Imagines you
threaten his manhood. Damages your self-esteem, demeans your growth, demands your silence.

7. Alcohol/drug abuse. Abuses alcohol/drugs.
Tries to get you drunk. Berates you if you won't
get high. He may deny his drug problem and
refuse to get help.

8. Difficulty expressing emotions. Unable to
identify feelings and express them directly and
appropriately. He may say he's hurt and sulk
when he's really angry. He displaces anger at
his boss or himself onto you.

9. Blames others for his feelings or problems. Believes others are out to get him and he's the victim. Blames you for everything that goes wrong. Will say "You make me mad," "You know which buttons to push" [and] "I can't help getting angry at you" to manipulate you. Holds you responsible for his suicidal or self-abusive behavior.

10. Hypersensitivity. Quick temper; unable to handle frustration without getting angry; easily insulted. Will rant and rave about minor things like traffic tickets or requests to do chores.

11. Dr. Jekyll and Mr. Hyde. Seems like two different people with mood swings from nice to explosive. May change his behavior around the guys. May be very sociable around others and only abusive with you. *yes LORD*

12. Unrealistic expectations. Very dependent on you for all his physical and emotional needs ("You're all I need"). Expects you to live up to his ideals of a perfect partner, mother, lover, friend.

13. Rigid sex roles. Expects a woman to stay at home, serve and obey him. Gets angry if you don't fulfill his wishes and anticipate his needs. Speaks for you. He thinks it's okay for men to keep women in line through intimidation. "The Ralph Cramden Syndrome."

14. Rigid religious beliefs. Justifies rigid sex roles and the physical/emotional/sexual domination of women and children with strict or distorted interpretations of Scripture.

15. Disrespect for women in general. Ridicules and insults women. Sees women as stupid and inferior to men. Tells sexist jokes. Refers to women in derogatory or non-human terms

(babe, chick, fox, bitch) or as specific parts of anatomy. Devalues women's accomplishments and work; acts like women are second-class citizens.

16. Emotional abuse. He may ignore your feelings, continually criticize you, and call you names like "fat," "ugly," and "stupid," curse and yell at you, belittle your accomplishments, manipulate you with lies, contradictions, and crazy-making tactics, humiliate you in private or in public, regularly threaten to leave or tell you to leave, keep you awake or wake you up to argue, or verbally abuse you.

17. Isolation. An acquaintance rapist will try to separate you from others to a secluded spot. Batterers will try to keep you from working or attending school, move you to a rural area, restrict your use of the phone or car. He will try to cut you off from other men, women, family, and children by saying things like "You're a whore," "You're a lesbian," "You're tied to your parent's apron strings," or "You're spoiling the kids."

18. Reliance on pornography. Rapists, child molesters, and men who sexually abuse or rape their wives often have an abundance of pornographic literature, photographs, magazines, or videos. They may want to involve you in their interest by photographing you or taking you to pornographic movies or shops.

19. Sexual abuse. Refuses platonic relationship if dating. Uses "playful" force in sex. Uses sulking or anger to manipulate you into having sex. Coerces or forces you to have sex or hurts you during sex. Demands sex when you're scared, ill, tired or starts having sex when you're asleep, drunk, or unable to give consent.

20. Cruelty to animals, children, or others. Teases, bullies, abuses, or harshly punishes animals, children, [the] elderly, weaker people, or other women. Is insensitive to other's pain. Tortures or kills pets to feel powerful or hurt you. Threatens to kidnap the children if you leave. Punishes or deprives children when he's angry at you. Punishes the children for behavior they're incapable of controlling (whipping a two year old for a wet diaper). Sixty percent of men who beat their wives also abuse their children.

21. Past Violence. Any history of violence with anyone to "solve" problems. Justifies hitting or abusing women in the past by saying "they made me do it." Friends, relatives, or ex-partners say he's abusive. (Batterers beat any woman they're with. You didn't cause it, and you can't control or cure it.)

22. Fascination with weapons. Plays with guns, knives, or other lethal weapons, threatens to get even with you or others.

23. Threats of violence. Any threats of physical force to control you or make you do something should be taken seriously. He may threaten to hurt you or your family. Non-batterers do not say things like "I'll break your neck" or "I'll kill you."

24. Breaking or striking objects. Punishes you by breaking objects you love. Terrorizes you into submission. If he doesn't want you to be a student, he may destroy your school books or break lamps. Non-batterers do not beat on tables, punch holes in walls, destroy furniture, throw objects at you to threaten you. The message is "You're next! You're just an object I can control and I can break you like I broke that."

25. Any force during an argument. Hurts you in anger or "in play," pushing, shoving, pulling, grabbing you by the collar, holding you down, restraining you from leaving the room, slapping, punching, hitting, kicking, or burning. This is the middle of the cycle of violence and will probably be followed by the honeymoon period then another period of escalating tension before the next violent episode. These episodes will get more frequent, more intense, and they will not stop on their own.

Worst Case Scenario

Consider this excerpt from the video *Battered* by Lee Grant:

> In the worst cases, battering may involve extreme physical or mental cruelty such as tying up the woman's hands and feet; beating her so badly that you break a shotgun in three pieces; stabbing her repeatedly so that she requires hundreds of stitches; cutting her throat; fracturing the roof of her mouth; and making cigarette burns in her breasts. Other batterers stalk and kill what they can no longer possess. These tragedies are usually portrayed as "crimes of passion" caused by the man's intense love for and inability to live without the woman. However, murder is actually the ultimate expression of the batterer's need to control the woman.

Dear Diary

Everything you need to know in order to determine whether you are living with abuse is in this chapter. You also know about denial now. Now is the time to break through the denial, admit you are abused, and get out. Remember that no one is going to rescue you.

Begin keeping a diary. Write down every hurtful thing your abuser says or does to you. Write down every name he calls you, every insult he hurls at you, every time he touches you or the children in anger or threatens to hurt one of you. If you have bruises or other injuries, have them photographed and keep the pictures with your diary. Keep it in a safe place where your abuser cannot possibly find it, even if that means giving it to a friend or family member for safekeeping after each entry.

We tend to forget the bad times when we long for the good, and we desperately want to believe our abusive partner when he says it will never happen again. Take your diary out and read it during those honeymoon phases. It will help you get and stay strong; it will make it easier to see through his lies and his empty promises. Read it often while you make decisions about your future.

If you haven't done so already, now is the time to contact your local battered women's program or shelter or the domestic violence coalition for your state. The telephone numbers are listed in Appendix B of this book. Call and make an appointment to talk with one of the counselors there. Take your diary with you so that you can share your experiences with the counselor if you are still in doubt as to whether or not your relationship with your partner is an abusive one.

The only courage that matters is the kind that
gets you from one minute to the next.
—Mignon McLaughlin

Let the ungodly fall into their own nets together:
and let me ever escape them.
—1662 Prayer Book

Invictus
by William Ernest Henley

Out of the night that covers me,
  Black as the pit from pole to pole,
I thank whatever gods may be,
  For my unconquerable soul.

In the fell clutch of circumstance
  I have not winced nor cried aloud.
Under the bludgeonings of chance
  My head is bloody but unbowed.

Beyond this place of wrath and tears
  Looms but the horror of the shade,
And yet the menace of the years
  Finds and shall find me unafraid.

It matters not how strait the gate
  How charged with punishments the scroll,
I am the master of my fate,
  I am the captain of my soul.

When nothing is sure, everything is possible.
—Margaret Drabble

Chapter Five

Making the Decision to Leave

You've Already Taken the First Step!

You know now that unless you take the first step—admitting you are abused, even if just to yourself—chances are you will continue to live in the abusive relationship until it bottoms out. That is, someone is badly hurt—or worse. Of course, it doesn't happen in every single case, but it happens in four million cases every year. And, in the unlikely case that your abusive relationship is one of the very few which never escalate to the point of physical injury or death, it will still be an abusive relationship and human beings cannot thrive in abusive relationships.

Remember that no one is going to rescue you. The justice system cannot help you, the medical profession cannot help you, and even your own family and friends cannot help you unless and until you say the words, "I am a battered woman. I want a better life for myself and my children. I am ready to get out of this violent relationship."

Even the battered women's shelters and domestic violence experts cannot help you until you identify yourself as a victim in need of assistance. They don't know who you are. They don't know where you are. They don't know what your needs are at this very moment. They stand able and eager to help you, but you have to let them know you need their help.

Ideally, by now you have answered the questions in the previous chapter and have determined whether you are indeed a victim of abuse. If you have determined that you are, you now have a critical decision to make. You have to decide whether to stay or go. It's a bitter pill, and I won't sugar-coat it. This may be the toughest decision you have ever made, and it may be the toughest you ever will make. But, it may also be the most important decision you ever make because it can mean the difference between life and death. At the very least, it is a decision that can determine whether you spend more days, weeks, months, and years being abused or whether you begin to find the peace and joy you deserve.

Most people, including the domestic violence experts and therapists who specialize in treating victims of abuse, will tell you, "It's your call. No one can make the decision to stay or go for you. You have to decide for yourself."

Truer words were never spoken. You are an intelligent human being and this is a free country. No one is going to make you leave your abusive husband or break up with your violent boyfriend. But, in making your decision, please consider the following.

Reality Check

First of all, if you are currently in a violent relationship, your perceptions almost certainly are distorted. Remember the story about the frog that boiled to death? He had adapted so gradually to the rising water temperature that he didn't notice when it got hot enough to kill him. Could you be like that little frog right now? Have you adapted to the gradually increasing violence in your life over so long a period

of time that you have simply failed to see how dangerous the situation has become? Are you minimizing your
pain, keeping a stiff upper lip, pretending things aren't
as bad as they are? If your answer is yes or maybe, it's
time to get out. If you don't know the answer, keep
reading.

Has your husband or boyfriend touched you in
anger, threatened to touch you in anger, thrown or
kicked something at you, or in any way made you fear
for your safety or the safety of your children? If he has,
it's time to get out.

Even if he has never touched you physically in
anger, does he insult you, call you names, yell at you,
blame everything that goes wrong on you, make fun of
you, put you down, cheat on you, lie to you, tell you
you are emotionally disturbed or crazy, or otherwise
hurt you emotionally over and over again and with less
and less remorse each time? Have these repeated verbal assaults left you feeling depressed and constantly
wondering what you're doing wrong and what you can
do to make him happy? Do you find yourself feeling
more frantic and more desperate to do better so that
he will love you again and stop being angry with you
all the time? Or does he "love" you so much and so
hard that it hurts you and makes you sad and scared?
Has the way he treats you made you feel so bad you
have considered killing yourself? If you have answered
yes to any of the questions in this paragraph, you are
a battered woman even if you have never had a mark
on your body. And, it's time to get out.

Remember that all domestic violence begins with
verbal abuse. Every incident of physical abuse is pre-
ceded by one or more incidents of verbal abuse. *The
violence will escalate*. It may be a year from now. It may
be next week. Or, it might happen tonight. No one
else may tell you this, but I will: it's time to get out.
Now.

What about Treatment Programs?

Secondly, you may have convinced yourself that if you can just get your partner into some kind of counseling or treatment program, the violence will end. Again, that is your call, but consider a few things.

The track record is not a good one for couples in violent relationships who enter into therapy with marriage counselors. In my own case, my first husband admitted our marriage was in serious trouble and, after much pleading on my part, agreed to go to a marriage counselor. The counselor was a good one and zeroed in on the problem after only a few sessions. He stated flatly that, although the marriage had a number of problems, the most serious and urgent appeared to be my husband's temper. Of course, Adam didn't want to hear that. "He's taking your side!" he yelled at me as we left the counselor's office one afternoon. "He's blaming everything on me!" And, he simply refused to go back again. I went a few more times by myself. The counselor pointed out to me that I had some serious decisions to make. I agreed, thanked him for his time, and went off to make my decisions.

Most stories I have heard about private counseling for couples when one of the partners is violent end in much the same way. The counselor identifies the problems of control, domination, and abuse; the abuser doesn't want to hear it; the abuser refuses to continue the counseling. Unless the counselor is one specifically trained in and exceptionally skilled at working with abusers, private counseling has little chance of success.

An anger management program is where an abuser belongs, but, sadly, there aren't nearly enough of these programs, and the track records of the existing programs are not great. Unless ordered to by the court and carefully followed for compliance, most abusive men do not cooperate with or complete these programs. More chilling than that, the recidivism rate (the rate of men who complete the program, then return to abusing their partners) is very high; even in the best programs in the country, the recidivism rate is greater than 50 percent. In other words, chances are that your abuser will not attend a treatment program and, even if he does, odds are he will batter you again.

Many victims of abuse think that Alcoholics Anonymous or a substance abuse treatment program is the answer because they mistakenly believe that alcohol and/or other drugs are responsible for their partner's violent behavior. "He only gets mean when he's been drinking" and "The only time he hits me is when he's high" are comments frequently made by battered women.

While it is true that a high percentage of abusers are alcoholics and/or drug abusers, the fact is that the abuse of alcohol and/or other drugs is an issue completely separate and apart from the issue of violence. Therefore, violent behavior and substance abuse require separate treatment programs. It may be that your partner could benefit from both kinds of programs, but his recovery is not your responsibility. Maybe he will get help and maybe he won't, but that decision is his to make. In the meantime, don't you make the mistake of thinking he will stop abusing you because he says he will join (or even has joined) Alcoholics Anonymous (AA) or enter a substance abuse treatment program. AA is a wonderful program for alcoholics, and many hospitals and treatment centers rely on the founding principles of AA in their own substance abuse programs, but those programs are there to help alcoholics and users of other drugs, not to treat people who are violent. The good people of AA would be the first to tell you that you didn't cause your partner's substance abuse, you can't control it, and you can't cure it. And, I'm here to tell you that the same holds true of your partner's abusive treatment of you.

Put Your Children First

Third, if you have children, they are suffering. If your husband or boyfriend is battering you either verbally or physically, your children are being abused simply by witnessing that violence. And, if your husband or boyfriend is battering *them* either verbally or physically, they are in immediate danger and it is your responsibility to get them safely out of their violent environment. Children who grow up as victims of abuse (and, again, they are victims whether the abuse is directed at them or they witness the abuse of their mother) typically exhibit poor impulse control, depression, low self-esteem, hopelessness, isolation from peers, and high risk for delinquent behaviors and extremely dangerous acts including sexual promiscuity, running away, alcohol/drug abuse, and suicide.

Other facts about the effects of family violence on children bear consideration:

- Children who live in violent homes are often injured unintentionally by thrown objects or when one partner wields a weapon against the other.
- Older children are often injured while attempting to protect their mothers.
- The long-term effects of family violence on children may include developmental delays, speech and language problems, learning difficulties, and stress-related physical disorders such as ulcers and headaches.
- Male children who witness domestic violence are more likely as adults to batter their female partners; female children who witness family violence are more likely to be abused as adults.

Gavin DeBecker, a personal security expert who helped write California's antistalking legislation, gave some straightforward advice during an interview on "Larry King Live" on 23 June 1994. "As hard as it is, leave," he said. "You are modeling for your children when you accept those blows. [When they are grown], your daughter will accept them, and your son will deliver them."

That's not what you want for your children. They deserve better. All of you deserve better. You didn't make your abuser abusive, and you can't change him. The only thing you can do is change yourself and change the environment in which you will raise your children. You want them to grow into healthy, strong, and confident adults who know how to trust and love and form lasting relationships with others. Violent households are unhealthy environments for everyone who lives in them, but the effects of the violence on the children may be especially long-lasting and crippling.

Many battered women find that making the decision to leave is just too difficult until they look at the effects of the violence on their children. If you are one of those women who is having trouble making the decision to leave in order to save yourself, then do it for your kids.

Don't make the mistake of saying, "I'm staying with him for the sake of the kids." If your relationship with your partner is a violent one, that's the worst thing you can do. "But the kids love him," you may say. "He's their father. They'll hate me if I take them away from him."

There is a very real possibility that the children may direct a lot of anger your way when you remove them from the family unit in which they have always lived, and it is a possibility you need to consider now so that you can be prepared for it. This is one of the many times when you are going to have to trust your judgment, know that you have made the right decision, and follow through on that decision.

If the children display anger toward you, know that it is probably fear of the unknown they are experiencing, fear of an uncertain and vastly different future from the one they had expected, and perhaps fear of more violence from your partner because you've left him. They may be sad and angry at the loss of this important man's presence in their home, especially if he is their father, and they may see the loss of his presence as your fault.

For many women who remove themselves and their children from violent relationships, this additional struggle with angry children is one of the most painful aspects. It certainly doesn't make the other struggles any easier, and only makes some of them more difficult. It may help if you understand that their anger is directed at you because you are the closest one to them (physically and emotionally) and because you are the safest person on whom they can unburden themselves. It's ironic, I know, but the reason they take it out on you is that they know they are safe with you. You will love them no matter what they do or say, and they know you will still be there when the dust settles. They are hurting and scared and, because they are children, they need to unload some of that, but it is up to you to see to it that their unloading is kept within reason. Don't overlook unacceptable behavior for any reason, least of all your own unwarranted feelings of guilt. Your children need limits now possibly more than at any other time in their lives because everything around them may seem so out of control right now. They need to know that you are steering the ship and that you have everything pretty well under control. Keep reminding yourself that, in the long run, this is the best move you can make for your children and for yourself.

Depending on their ages, your children may display their anxiety in different ways, and it may be necessary to get one or all of them into counseling right away if the symptoms you observe go beyond the usual ones of sadness and anger. Withdrawal from family and friends, aggression, lack of appetite, sleep disturbances, and other obvious signs of poor health indicate an immediate need for an evaluation of a child by a pediatrician who can then make further recommendations if necessary. Older children—and especially male adolescents—who begin to behave violently themselves require immediate professional intervention and counseling.

On the other hand, you may find that your children (especially the older ones) do not have a problem with the change in family structure, but rather are supportive of the decisions you have made even though, like you, they are saddened by the shifting family unit and frightened of what the future may hold. They may experience enormous relief that the violence in their lives is ending. This is often the case when the violence has been especially severe and destructive and when family members have been injured by the abuser.

Now You're Ready

Before going any further, I want to emphasize the enormous progress you have made just by having read this far and considered the material presented here. It took a lot of courage for you to pick up this book in the first place and to admit that it might contain information helpful to you. It has taken more courage for you to keep reading, answering the questions, and thinking about what your answers mean.

Now you're ready to get out. You are ready to end the violence once and for all, for you and for your children. You want to discover for yourself what a great big beautiful world there is out there waiting for you to come get your piece of it. I promise you that what you're looking for is out there somewhere. Don't allow your vision of your future to be clouded by the experiences in your past. The world is a beautiful place, and it is filled with many warm and wonderful people who want to know you. It's full of fun things to do, places to explore, and more things to learn about than you have ever imagined. But, you have to get out to get there.

Before you go to bed, give your troubles to God.
He'll be up all night anyway.

—Source Unknown

If you don't feel close to God,
guess who moved?

—Source Unknown

The Road Not Taken
by Robert Frost

Two roads diverged in a yellow wood,
And sorry I could not travel both
And be one traveler, long I stood
And looked down one as far as I could
To where it bent in the undergrowth;

Then took the other, as just as fair,
And having perhaps the better claim,
Because it was grassy and wanted wear;
Though as for that the passing there
Had worn them really about the same,

And both that morning equally lay
In leaves no step had trodden black.
Oh, I kept the first for another day!
Yet knowing how way leads on to way,
I doubted if I should ever come back.

I shall be telling this with a sigh
Somewhere ages and ages hence:
Two roads diverged in a wood, and I—
I took the one less traveled by,
And that has made all the difference.

I steer my boat with hope, leaving fear astern.

—Thomas Jefferson

Chapter Six

Getting Out

Personal Safety Plan

The first thing you must do is carefully formulate a personal safety plan. At the end of this book, you will find a suggested format for this plan (appendix A). If this book belongs to you and you have somewhere to keep it where it is absolutely safe from the eyes of others, go ahead and write your answers on the safety plan pages. Be very careful never to leave your safety plan where your abuser can find it. You don't want him to know where to come looking for you after you leave. If this book doesn't belong to you or if you choose not to write in it for other reasons, photocopy the pages of the safety plan or copy them in your own hand into a notebook. However you choose to do it, guard these pages carefully. They are for your eyes only, unless you choose to have a friend, family member, or battered women's advocate review them with you or even have a copy of them for safekeeping.

Planning a Safe Escape

Ideally, once you have made the decision to leave your abusive relationship, you will have some time in which to plan your escape. Please don't try to force this time. If it isn't there, it just isn't there. It is much more important for you and your children to be physically safe than to have every detail arranged. But, if you do have the time to plan, here are some tips to guide you.

• Know the telephone number of the nearest battered women's shelter or a domestic violence hotline. *Memorize it*. Also, write it down and put it in your wallet or purse.

• Call the local domestic violence hotline to get information about local laws, shelters, and other resources available to you. Don't wait for a crisis and don't wait until you leave to get this information. Get it now and keep it in a safe place where your abuser cannot find it.

• Apply for credit cards in your own name.

• Open a checking or savings account *in your name only* and transfer funds to the new account. Use a different bank from the one you and your abuser may have used together.

• Get a post office box. Fill out change of address forms so that your mail will be forwarded to the post office box.

• Plan several escape routes leading away from your house. If your abuser follows you, it may be necessary to do some evasive driving. Knowing your way around and knowing several ways of getting to your intended destination may come in handy.

• Plan where you will go. Keep in mind that your abuser will look for you first at the homes of relatives and friends; therefore, those may not be safe places. Your safest bet is your contact with a battered women's shelter. If you live in a rural area or a community where no shelter exists, consider whether you can safely drive the distance necessary to reach such a shelter. Telephone ahead and let them know to expect you. They may have other suggestions and may even be able to send someone to meet you. If none of these options is possible, consider temporarily checking into a motel or hotel. If your abuser follows you and you feel threatened, *do not hesitate to call the police* and tell them you are in danger.

• Have an extra set of car keys and some cash hidden in the car. Have another set of car keys, keys to your home, and cash stored at the home of a trusted friend or relative.

• Plan the safest time to leave.

• These are important items you must take with you or have stored with a friend or relative ahead of time: a change of clothes for you and for each child; toilet articles (toothbrushes, a comb, deodorant, etc.) and prescription drugs; car registration and driver's license, extra cash, checkbook and savings account passbook; medical records (especially children's immunization records), birth certificates, social security cards, insurance papers (both car and health), welfare papers and immigration papers *for you and the children.* If you can't take or store these ahead of time because your abuser might notice they are missing, photocopy them and put the originals back. The photocopies will serve your needs for the foreseeable future.

• It is also a good idea to rent a safety deposit box at the bank. You can put the important papers listed above in this box well in advance of your leaving, and it's also an ideal place to keep evidence of abuse, your diary and a copy of your safety plan. Be sure to keep the key to your safety deposit box with you at all times.

• Take legal papers such as divorce decrees, records of police complaints, income tax returns, adoption papers, marriage license, children's school records, professional licenses, diplomas, etc.

• Take something special for each child, such as a favorite toy or blanket.

• Take something special for yourself, such as photograph albums or other treasured items.

• Take your pets if possible or make sure you have a place for them. Board them temporarily with your veterinarian if necessary, or ask a friend or relative to care for them until you are relocated. Remember that abusive men sometimes torture and/or kill pets to terrorize their partners or punish them for leaving.

• If it is necessary to the safety of you and your children to leave the area and travel some distance, take with you small, salable items such as television sets, cameras, jewelry, radios, art pieces, or other objects which can be sold or traded for necessities.

• Tell someone you trust that you are leaving, when you are leaving, and where you are going. If you do not have someone you can trust with this information, call the domestic abuse hotline number or battered women's shelter number and give this information to that agency.

• When it's time to leave, call the police if you think your abuser or someone else may try to stop you or if you think you may be in danger.

• Set a deadline and *go*. You know enough now to know that things are not going to get better if you stay.

It may be necessary to keep this information temporarily from your own children, especially the youngest ones, because they may not understand the concept of keeping a secret, even when their own safety is at stake. This doesn't mean you must lie to them. Tell them that you and they are going to visit friends or take a ride in the car.

Other Considerations

• If you cannot take pets with you or make arrangements for their care, leave food and water out for them. As soon as you are at a safe location, let someone know the pets need care.

• Do not leave a note for your abuser. You may feel like you should leave him some kind of note to

explain that you are leaving and why. Resist the temp-
tation. He will know you have gone soon enough, and
he knows why without your telling him. You don't owe
him an explanation. You don't owe him anything.

• Do not leave behind scribbled notes, doodles,
business cards, shelter information, travel information
(airline, bus, or train schedules). You would be surprised at the use your abuser can make of these clues
to your whereabouts.

• Take food and water with you, snacks for the
children, formula, and other infant needs.

• Hide weapons, dispose of them, and/or dispose
of ammunition.

• Move furniture and other large belongings into
a storage facility. You can come back for them when
you are settled once again.

If You Have Decided to Stay or Can't Get Out

Of course, I hope you have made the decision to
leave your abusive relationship and are ready to get
out. But, I know that many readers will not be ready
to make these decisions or will, perhaps, leave the
relationship and come back. I did it myself several
times. Battered women's advocates tell us that victims
leave their abusers an average of three to six times
before making the final break.

Don't blame yourself or be embarrassed. Know that
it is all part of the process of separating from someone
who, for all his faults, has been an important person in
your life. You may still love him very much. Don't
listen to people who tell you how you should or
shouldn't feel. Even if it could be done, no one has the
right to dictate your feelings. For reasons having to do
with love and for reasons you may not even be able to
identify, you may return to your abuser over and over
again.

Please know that the staff of your local battered women's shelter or program know all of this better than anyone. Don't ever think *I couldn't possibly face them again.* No one there is going to criticize or blame you or shake their heads in puzzlement if you decide to stay or if you leave and go back. Each time you leave, they will be ready, waiting, and eager to help you again. Each time you go back, they will counsel you on staying safe. All they care about is your safety and the safety of your children.

Know that this is your decision, but keep in mind the important facts you have already learned: there will be a "honeymoon" phase, the violence will eventually erupt again, and the next time will probably be worse.

If you decide to stay, or if you leave and come back, please stay safe. The following information may help.

How to Respond to Verbal Abuse

Patricia Evans (*The Verbally Abusive Relationship* [Holbrook: Bob Adams, Inc. , 1992], 132) offers the following suggestions for you to keep in mind when responding to verbal abuse:

- Know that when you are being put down, ordered around, yelled at and so forth, you are being abused. And abuse is unjust, disabling, and destructive.

- Remember that the abuser is not speaking in a rational, adult way.

- Know that you are responding to a person who is in some way trying to control, dominate, or establish superiority over you.

- Know that you have done nothing to cause it.

- *Know that it is not healthy to live in an abusive atmosphere* (emphasis mine).

> • Distance yourself from the abuser by seeing his immaturity for what it is.

> • Respond with a tone of authority and firmness that shows that you mean business, are serious, and will not tolerate any more abuse.

> • Stay aware. Concentrate on the *present*. Notice what *your* senses tell you. How do *you* feel? How does he sound to *you*? What do you see?

Safety during a Violent Incident

If you have decided to stay, have left and returned, or if you have made the decision to leave but are still in the process of making your plans, know that another physically violent incident can occur at any time. If your abuser has learned that you are planning to leave him, this can be a particularly dangerous time for you. Many abusers become enraged when they discover their partners are leaving them, and it is at this time that the greatest potential for life-threatening violence exists. For this reason, it is essential that you tell no one of your plans other than those who will be instrumental in helping you escape.

Here are some strategies to think about ahead of time in anticipation of another violent incident.

• Don't get backed into the bathroom, kitchen, garage, or other rooms where there are sharp corners and objects which can be used as weapons. If there are weapons in the house, try to avoid movement toward their locations.

• Have several escape routes from the house. Don't get backed into a room with no exit to the outside.

• Have a "secret code" word with at least one of your children. When he or she hears you say that word, it is a signal to call the police or slip out the door and go for help. Tell that child ahead of time exactly where and to whom he is to go for help should the need arise. Tell him to take younger siblings with him if possible and to stay at the designated location until you come for him. Under no circumstances should the children return to the house during a violent incident or become involved in the physical violence. Your children must understand that their job is to stay safe, *not* to take care of you.

• Have a signal arranged with the children that tells them not to come in the house. For example, if the front porch light is on when they come home from school, they are to go to a neighbor's house and summon help. They should also know to go to a neighbor's if they approach your house and hear sounds of violence.

• If possible, have a designated "safe room" in the house. This room should have a telephone and a sturdy bolt lock on the inside of the door. Children should be taught to go to this room, lock the door, and call the police if it is impossible to leave when an argument escalates to violence. Go into this room with them unless doing so might increase the danger to them.

• If your children are old enough, rehearse with them what they are to do in an emergency. Practice leaving with them as if you were having a fire drill.

• If you have a neighbor whom you trust and who lives within hearing distance, speak frankly with her (or him). Ask that she call the police if she hears noises coming from your home that could indicate violence.

• Arrange a signal with a neighbor that will let her know to call you and see if everything is all right. The signal could be a window shade pulled all the way down, the porch light off when it would otherwise be on, or some other detail out of its usual place. Have a code word arranged with her. If you use that word when she calls you, that is her signal to call the police.

• If you have a car, get into the habit of backing it into the driveway or otherwise parking it so that you don't have to put it in reverse or turn the car around to leave. Keep the gas tank full at all times.

• Keep cash and car keys where they can be easily grabbed in the event you must leave quickly.

• *Take your children with you.* Even in an emergency situation, leaving them may result in charges against you for child endangerment or abandonment.

• If you cannot escape, it may be possible to stop the attack by pretending to faint. Try to stay calm and *use your head.* Outsmart him if you can't outmaneuver him.

• Keep any physical evidence of the incident. Physical evidence includes but is not limited to torn clothing, bruises and/or injuries to you or the children (have someone you trust photograph these injuries as soon as possible and twenty-four hours later and again forty-eight hours later and/or write a description of them, or have a physician document them; keep photos with a friend or in a safety deposit box at a bank), and broken furniture and damaged walls (take photos of these and safeguard them).

• If you or the children are injured, go to the emergency room or your family doctor. Insist that the injuries be documented as well as your and the children's explanations of how the injuries were received.

When the Police Are Called

Anytime you are in danger or fear for your safety or that of your children, call the police or have one of the children or someone else call the police. In spite of the fact that some law enforcement officials have not received the comprehensive training they need in order to understand the dynamics of domestic violence, the police are still your first line of defense when you are in danger and you should never hesitate to call them.

Ginny NiCarthy offered numbers one to nine of the following suggestions for getting the most effective police response in her book *Getting Free* (Seattle: Seal Press [1982], 79); the rest are my additions.

1. Be as calm as you possibly can be.
2. Don't be afraid to ask the police to make a report.
3. Tell them about the assault in detail.
4. Show them any injuries or bruises or damaged property.
5. Let them know if there are any witnesses.
6. Tell them about other violent incidents.
7. Show them any court documents you have such as no contact or restraining orders.
8. Ask them for community resources such as shelters, hotlines, counseling, and advocacy.
9. Ask for the case number of the report and a phone number if you want to follow up on the case.
10. Ask to speak to them outside the presence of your abuser.
11. Ask if an officer or other official can photograph your injuries immediately and again in twenty-four to forty-eight hours. Some injuries—especially bruises—will not show up right away.
12. Do not allow police officers to minimize the assault. If you feel they have, go to the police station as soon as you are able and ask to speak to the officers' supervisor. Describe your experience to him or her. If you still do not think the incident has been properly addressed, ask the legal advocate at your local battered women's shelter for advice on how to proceed.

Will My Abuser Be Arrested?

Generally speaking, police officers can make an arrest if they have probable cause to believe a crime has been committed and that someone was injured during the commission of that crime. Probable cause usually requires some physical evidence of injury to the victim. Laws vary from state to state, however, and there are many variables. Some jurisdictions now have mandatory arrest policies which require that abusers be arrested (this is a move in the right direction, but has been known to backfire when officers arrest the victim for defending herself), and some have pro-arrest policies which favor arresting the abuser. You need to contact the legal advocate at a battered women's program or your local legal aid society (phone numbers for these are in Appendix B at the end of this book) and find out what the arrest policies are where you live.

NiCarthy and other experts tell us the likelihood that your abuser will be arrested increases if there are outstanding warrants against him, if you or one of your children has been seriously injured, if your abuser is wielding a weapon or used a weapon in his assault on you or your children, or if he continues his assault on you in the presence of the police or attacks them.

If it appears that no arrest will be made—or if an arrest is made but your abuser will be released within a few hours or even days—you should plan to stay somewhere else for at least awhile. Tell your abuser you feel the two of you need a cooling-off period if he is not being arrested, then ask the police officers to see you safely to a battered women's shelter or the home of a friend or relative, or ask them to stay until you have left. Make it very clear to them that you do not believe you will be safe if they leave you alone with your abuser.

Following any incident of physical abuse (whether or not the police were called) and as soon as you are at a safe location, speak to a battered women's advocate. Describe this most recent abusive incident and request information on filing charges against your abuser. Requirements can be very different from one locality to another, and laws are being updated all the time. Your local battered women's program staff will have the most recent information and will be able to guide you.

If you are able to file charges against your abuser, do it and follow through. Only when victims consistently bring charges against their abusers, and follow through on them regardless of the consequences, will the abusers and the legal system begin to get the message that we will not be victims anymore. Your voice is important, and your story counts.

Prayer for This House
by Louis Untermeyer

*May nothing evil cross this door,
And may ill fortune never pry
About these windows; may the roar
    And rain go by.*

*Strengthened by faith, these rafters will
Withstand the batt'ring of the storm;
This hearth, though all the world grow chill,
    Will keep us warm.*

*Peace shall walk softly through these rooms,
Touching our lips with holy wine,
Till every casual corner blooms
    Into a shrine.*

*Laughter shall drown the raucous shout;
And though these shelt'ring walls are thin,
May they be strong to keep hate out
    And hold love in.*

Chapter Seven

Staying Safe

It's Not Over Yet

I wish I could tell you that, once you have suc-ceeded in escaping your abuser, he will leave you alone and you and your children will be safe from him for-ever. Unfortunately, this is not usually the case. Your abuser may react with shock and surprise that you have taken this step away from him, or he may be-come enraged that you have left him. Either reaction can spell trouble, and you need to be prepared.

The most likely scenario is one in which your abuser will act totally surprised that you have made this move and try to lure you back with promises that "it will never happen again." He may tell you that you have really made an impression on him this time, that he hadn't realized how miserably unhappy his behavior had made you, and that you are absolutely right when you say he needs counseling of some kind. He may promise to enter an anger-management program. He may cry and break your heart with his pleas. He may suggest that the two of you begin to date one another again, that you give your relationship a new begin-ning. I have seen dramatic cases where the abuser has sent his victim luxury airfare tickets to romantic, far-away destinations where he vows the two of them will fall in love all over again. In other cases, abusers have promised to buy something the victim has always longed for, such as a house, a car, acres of waterfront property, and so on. After I left my abuser, he played a scaled-down variation of this game for awhile by asking me out on dates, sending me romantic cards in the mail and giving the children gifts to bring to me.

Remember that you always have the option of going back, but also *remember that you have been in this place before*, even if on a smaller scale. If you fall for these promises, you will be right back in the cycle of violence. There will be a period of moonlight, roses and romance (the "honeymoon period"), then the tension will begin to build again until it erupts in another violent incident—one that is likely to be more severe than any that have gone before. You will be right back where you started, possibly with serious injuries this time. And maybe worse.

If you find yourself wavering about your decision to leave, call a friend or relative who supports the decision you have made. Call the battered women's program nearest you, even if you have not made contact with that organization before. The people there will help you to renew your resolve and will be able to offer suggestions for getting through this difficult period.

If you began keeping a diary as suggested in chapter 4, now is a good time to take it out and review the history of this relationship. If you have photos of your injuries or of property damage, look at them again.

The period of time right after leaving the relationship is a dangerous time for victims of domestic violence because many abusers become enraged upon discovering their partners have left them. Others spend considerable time, energy, and money as described above, trying to lure their victims back, then erupt into violence when their efforts to persuade them to return fail. Either way, you can expect that he will attempt to get you into a situation where he can control, intimidate, violate, and abuse you again. The difference now, of course, is that you are in control. The trick is to keep your guard up and maintain that control.

One way of maintaining control is to turn down his requests to meet him somewhere to talk things over. Be firm. Tell him there is nothing to discuss. If there is something that requires discussion, tell him that he can discuss it with you (by phone or in writing) through your attorney, through a counselor at the battered women's shelter, or through some other advocate who will ensure your privacy and safety. Do not agree to let him come to where you are now living. That is nothing more than an invitation to trouble.

If at all possible, do not let him know where you are living. If you have started divorce or separation proceedings and he has been given visitation rights with the children, meet him at a public place to deliver and pick up the children; there is almost certainly nothing in your separation agreement or divorce decree that says anything about him picking them up at your home.

Do not let him have your telephone number and keep your number unlisted and unpublished. Visitation arrangements can be on a regularly scheduled basis so that phone calls aren't necessary; messages about emergency changes in plans can be delivered through a third party. Be very careful of who you give your telephone number to, as he may be able to wheedle it out of someone else. If he gets your new number, change it. Change it again if necessary. If he continues to get your telephone numbers, invest in a caller identification service from your telephone company or use an answering machine to screen your phone calls. If your abuser leaves messages on the answering machine, save the message tapes as possibly valuable evidence.

Mark the tapes with the dates and the times of the phone calls if you know that information.

Safety in Your House

Much of the following information is from the comprehensive series of brochures published by the Crime Prevention Unit of the Norfolk Police Department (Norfolk, Virginia) in the interest of public safety. Use these tips and any additional ones which may be offered by the police or sheriff's department in your community.

It is essential that you make your home safe from *all* possible intruders, but especially from your abuser. In most communities, you can call the police department and arrange for an officer to come to your home and conduct a security survey. The officer will point out areas of concern and offer suggestions for improving the security of your residence. In the meantime, there is plenty you can do.

If your neighborhood has organized a Neighborhood Watch program (it may go by a different name in your community), be sure the participating members know of your situation. If your neighborhood doesn't have such a program, think about starting one. Your local police department can provide you with organizational information.

Check out the exterior of your home to be sure you haven't inadvertently provided hiding places or easy access to your home for those you don't want entering it. Trim shrubbery so that the view to and from every window and door is clear and open and so that there are no hidden corners where someone can lie in wait for you. You want to be able to see your front door and windows when you arrive home, and you want neighbors and patrolling police officers to be able to see anyone lurking about. Also, keep large trees near the house pruned in such a way that limbs cannot be used to gain access to upper floors.

Make sure your house number is easily visible from the street so that emergency personnel can respond quickly if necessary. It's a good idea to have the number on the front of the house itself and near the street or on the curb in front of the house. Use fluorescent or white paint and metal or glow-in-the-dark numbers which can be purchased at the hardware store.

Doors

All exterior doors should be made of solid wood or steel, not the type with hollow centers. Hollow doors are easily smashed in with heavy tools. They offer little or no security.

Change the locks! Whether or not you believe your abuser has a key to your residence, have a qualified and bonded locksmith install new locks on all exterior doors. Do not waste money on inferior locks. You want a lock with a minimum one-inch bolt throw, free-spinning beveled cylinder guards constructed of case-hardened steel, one-fourth inch case-hardened bolts which hold the two cylinder halves together, and a five-pin tumbler.

A doorknob lockset should have an anti-shim device which is a spring-latch with a small horizontal pin which keeps the latch from being retracted when the door is closed. Anything of lesser quality can be opened easily by just about anyone who wants to get into your home badly enough.

In addition to the doorknob lock, you should have a deadbolt lock with a one-inch throw. The metal plate attached to your door jamb or frame for the purpose of receiving the bolt is called the strike plate. Periodically check this plate to make sure it is solidly in place.

Double cylinder deadlocks are deadbolt locks which provide for the use of a key on both sides of the door. These locks are especially desirable on doors containing glass within forty inches of the lock. If an intruder breaks the glass, he will not be able to unlock the door by reaching through the space where the glass was. For the sake of safety, keep a key to the deadbolt lock on a nail inside and near the door, but far enough away that it cannot be reached by someone breaking through the glass from the outside. Children should know how to get this key and open this lock in the event of an emergency such as a fire.

Have wide-angle viewers (peepholes) installed in all exterior doors. Your locksmith may offer this service but, if not, now is the time for you to learn to do some things you may always have considered "guy things," such as learning to use a drill. Ask your hardware dealer for advice and instructions. Borrow or rent tools if you can't afford to buy them.

(I promise you will feel enormous pride and satisfaction when you begin taking these steps to take care of yourself and your children. Among the proudest moments of my life were my first Christmas Eve alone when I put together a Big Wheel and a bike with training wheels all by myself and the time I repaired my vacuum cleaner. Those may not seem like big deals to a lot of people, but they were to me. I had never handled screwdrivers and wrenches. Learning to use tools was one of the many small things that helped me truly believe I was going to make it on my own and be able to take care of my sons and myself.)

If any of the exterior doors to your home open outward, they are a security risk. Anyone who wants to gain entry to your home only has to remove the hinge pins to remove this type of door. Replace these doors as soon as possible. If you cannot afford to do that, you can alter the door yourself. Insert a framing nail or screw into the back edge of the door midway between the top and center door hinges and another nail or screw midway between the center and the bottom door hinges. Leave these two nails or screws protruding at

least one-half inch. Drill two holes opposite these two
nails or screws to receive them when the door is closed.
When this is done, the hinge pins may still be removed
from the outside, but the door will be held firmly in
place.

Don't overlook the garage door and other possible
points of entry into your home. Ask your hardware
dealer to recommend steel hasps and padlocks for the
garage door. If your garage has windows that are usually kept shut, go ahead and nail them shut. Other
openings to your home which require your attention
include ventilation openings, crawlspaces beneath the
house, and swinging doors used by pets. Secure these
access points by installing grilles, heavy screening, or
locks. "Bowser" will have to be retrained to request
exit and entry! It may be convenient for him to have
his own door, but it's not safe for the rest of the family.

Sliding glass doors (and windows) can be secured
so that they cannot be opened or lifted from their
tracks even when the locks have been broken or removed. Rev up your drill and make at least a one-
quarter inch (in diameter) hole that angles downward
through the top channel and continues into the top
portion of the sliding door or window frame when
closed. By placing a solid metal bolt or pin into the
hole, the door or window will be secured. When not in
use, the bolt or pin can be attached to a cord and
dropped through a screw-eye adjoining the door or
window.

Additional security can be provided by screwing
two or three no. 8 or no. 10 sheet metal screws into the
track above a sliding door. The screws should pro-
trude so the top of the closing door clears them. This
will prevent the door from being lifted out of the lower
track. Pin-type locks are inexpensive and are easily
installed to prevent the operation of sliding glass doors.

Windows

Casement windows (the crank type) are easy to secure by replacing any hardware that is old or worn. Make sure the lock works properly and the crank has no excessive play in it. Louver-type windows, on the other hand, are difficult to secure because the individual panes of glass are easy to remove. Application of a two-part epoxy resin to each pane of glass along the metal retaining strip will prevent easy removal. The use of grilles or grates is recommended for louvered windows. If window grilles or grates are installed in bedrooms, be sure they are designed to open from the inside to reduce the risk of being trapped in the event of a fire.

Double-hung sash-type windows are easy to secure with key locks from the hardware store or a locksmith. A do-it-yourself security measure is to drill a hole into the top window approximately five or six inches from the top of the window (the amount you want to be able to leave the window open) and another hole in the bottom window that will match the hole on the top window when the window is opened the desired amount. Inserting pins (nails or screws) through these matching holes secures the window in the open position which allows for ventilation and prevents the window from being opened any farther by someone on the outside.

Please remember that one window in every room on every floor must be available for use as a fire exit. Bedroom windows may often be the safest and quickest means of escaping a house fire during the night. Be sure that any burglar bars or other type of metal grilles or bars on windows are easily opened from the inside. Consult with your hardware dealer or locksmith for the best window security for your situation.

Be sure to close the blinds, pull down the shades,

and draw the drapes and curtains in the evening or any time you feel uncomfortable.

Other Safety Measures

Exterior lighting is one of your best and least expensive security investments. The front, sides, and rear of your home should be well-lighted. Install outside floodlights just below the eaves of the roof and cover them with wire mesh to prevent the intentional breakage of the bulbs. Use exterior lights with sensors which automatically turn them on and off or attach a timer.

Electronic security systems range in price from relatively inexpensive to outrageous. Look into these systems, but if you decide to purchase one, buy from a reputable company. Check them out first. If you are afraid of getting ripped off, ask someone you trust who knows more about home security than you do, such as your hardware store manager or a police officer. Sometimes the most effective home security device is a dog with a loud bark (or even just a big pet dish on the front porch with something like "Killer" or "Cujo" written on it!) or a sticker on the front door which says the house is protected by an electronic system. Don't overlook these simple, inexpensive suggestions if you can't afford more sophisticated security, but do purchase the best security you can afford, even if it means borrowing money from relatives or friends. Your life and the lives of your children are worth every penny.

If you are living in an apartment complex where laundry facilities are shared, consider arranging to go with a neighbor to and from the laundry room. Likewise for mailrooms and parking garages.

If your door has a mail slot, attach an interior hood over the slot which will prevent anyone from looking through the slot into your house, but will not interfere with mail delivery.

You should have a smoke alarm on every floor of your home and one in every bedroom. Make sure all the smoke alarms are working. Check the batteries frequently. Keep fire extinguishers in the kitchen and garage and one in your bedroom. Use the test function on the extinguisher to check it frequently. Abusers who are unable to gain entry have been known to start fires.

Purchase a cellular telephone, even if you have to borrow the money to do it. It will give you an added measure of security wherever you go, but it is especially important to keep it by your bed at night. If the telephone lines to your home are cut, you will still be able to call the police.

Keep a list of important telephone numbers taped next to every phone in the house. *Every child should be taught to dial 911 and to give his name and address.* Most large communities now have enhanced 911 systems which automatically show the dispatcher the caller's location, but some rural areas and smaller communities are still without this system.

Talk to your children, baby-sitters and neighbors about when and under what circumstances they should call the police. Unless firmly cautioned ahead of time, a baby-sitter (especially a teen-ager) can be easily duped by your ex-partner's offer to pay her and send her home while he stays with the children. Unless told what to look for, neighbors might easily ignore a man knocking on your door who shouldn't be there. And, unless told (often repeatedly!) not to, small children are easily conned into opening the door to your ex-partner, especially if he is their father.

Our legal system is far from perfect, and abusers often have visitation rights with their children, rights which abusers use more often than not simply to gain access to their former partners. If he follows the typical pattern, your abuser will take advantage of every opportunity to get you into a position where he can gain control of you once again, and visitation rights are one of the easiest ways for him to do that. Don't let him! As mentioned earlier, you can arrange to meet him with the children in a public place for him to pick them up for visits and return them to you, but if he does come to your home at visitation times, you answer the door when he arrives to pick up the children. Do not allow him to come in no matter what the excuse. And, lock the door securely once he's gone.

Work out a signal with a neighbor which will tell him or her that you need help. A window shade opened all the way or a porch light off at night can be a signal to call you to see if you are okay. Arrange a code word which, if used during the phone call, alerts the neighbor to call the police. And, of course, the neighbor is to call the police if you do not answer the phone and he or she is fairly certain you are home.

Relatives and close friends should be asked to call you frequently and ask if you are alright. They, too, should know your code word. If you are on the phone with them and use the code word, they are to hang up and call the police.

Notify your family members and friends, the children's schools, and your church that you and your partner no longer live together and that your ex-partner is not allowed to pick the children up.

Reread chapter 6. Learn and be ready to use the appropriate measures recommended under "Safety During a Violent Incident" and "Safety If You Have Time to Plan Your Escape."

Safety Away from Your Home

In my home state, a stalker is defined as "any person who on more than one occasion engages in conduct directed at another person with the intent to place, or with the knowledge that the conduct places, that other person in reasonable fear of death, criminal sexual assault, or bodily injury to that other person or to that other person's spouse or child." Some states have broader definitions which include a wider range of behaviors. You can request a copy of your state's stalking legislation by calling the office of your state representative. You can also contact a legal aid organization or a legal advocate for battered women to find out if your abuser's behaviors constitute stalking. If his behaviors meet the criteria for stalking in your state, I urge you to bring charges against him and follow through on them.

Change your routine if you even *think* your abuser is stalking you. Change the times and days you go to the grocery store and the bank. Go to church services at different times. If possible, ask to be put on a different shift or schedule at work. Analyze all the activities you do in the course of a day, and plan to do them differently in the days to come.

Keep your diary updated. Make note of every time you feel threatened or in the least bit unsafe because of your abuser's behavior. Keep evidence of his stalking behaviors (notes left on your car, strange or scary items sent to you in the mail, etc.).

If you haven't already, begin establishing a paper trail. Call the police and file a report every time your abuser threatens you or engages in stalking behaviors or approaches you and begins to verbally or physically assault you. Make your own notes about every such encounter and every contact with the police. Keep this information with your diary and other evidence. You may never need it or use it, but then again, it might save your life one day when it convinces a judge to put your abuser behind bars.

Take a class in self-defense. Not only will you feel more confident in your ability to take care of yourself, but these classes are great exercise for your mind and your body.

Never leave a note on your door for anyone telling them where you've gone or when you will be back. Your abuser would love to have that information.

When driving, keep your car doors locked and the windows rolled up far enough to prevent someone from reaching inside. Stay alert when you stop for traffic signs and lights. Keep your eyes moving around the outside of the car, and keep the car in gear. If your abuser (or anyone!) tries to force you off the road or stop you, honk your horn and drive away as quickly as is safely possible. Go immediately to a public place, blowing your horn all the way. Whoever is harassing you will more than likely give up the chase at this point. Whatever you do, don't go home. He will follow you there and you will be in danger.

If you drive to work each day, take different routes on different days. Mix them up. Travel well-lit, busy streets. Don't be predictable.

Don't leave your car unlocked, even for a few minutes. That's an invitation to your abuser to wait for you in your car. Have your keys in your hand when you approach your car so that you don't have to fumble for them. Keys can also be used as a weapon if you are attacked. Keep a small flashlight attached to your key ring so you can check around, inside, and underneath your car before getting into it.

When you arrive home, look around at your house and yard before exiting your car. If you have a garage, the cost of a remote control garage door opener and automatic lights is money well-spent. If any of the doors or windows appear to have been tampered with, get back in your car, drive to a safe location, and call the police.

If you use public transportation, avoid isolated bus stops. Stay near other passengers and/or the driver. If your abuser boards the bus, tell the driver you are in danger. He can request police assistance by radio.

Be sure that your employer and co-workers are aware of what is going on. Ask if a colleague can screen your telephone calls at work. Ask a security guard or other employees to escort you to and from the parking area.

If You Fear for Your Life

Some experts say it is impossible to determine whether a batterer is likely to kill. Still others offer the following guidelines. Study them carefully.

1. *Threats of homicide or suicide.* The batterer who has threatened to kill himself, his partner, the children, or her relatives must be considered extremely dangerous.

2. *Fantasies of homicide or suicide.* The more the batterer has developed a fantasy about who, how, when, and/or where to kill, the more dangerous he may be. The batterer who has previously acted out part of a homicide or suicide fantasy may be invested in killing as a viable solution to his problems.

3. *Depression.* Where a batterer has been acutely depressed and sees little hope for moving beyond the depression, he may be a candidate for homicide and suicide.

4. *Weapons.* When a batterer possesses weapons and has used them or threatened to use them in the past in his assaults on the battered woman, the children, or himself, his access to those weapons increases his potential for lethal assault.

5. *Obsessiveness about a partner or family.* A man who is obsessive about his female partner, who either idolizes her and feels that he cannot live without her, or believes he is entitled to her no matter what because she is his wife, is more likely to be life-endangering.

6. *Centrality of the battered woman.* If the loss of the battered woman represents or precipitates a total loss of hope for a positive future, a batterer may choose to kill.

7. *Rage.* The most life-endangering rage often erupts when a batterer believes the battered woman is leaving him or after she has left him.

8. *Drug or alcohol consumption.* Consumption of drugs or alcohol when in a state of despair or fury can elevate the risk of lethality.

9. *Pet abuse.* Those batterers who assault and mutilate pets are more likely to kill or maim family members.

10. *Access to the battered woman and/or family members.* If the batterer cannot find her, he cannot kill her.

If you determine that your abuser is likely to commit life-endangering violence, you must take extraordinary measures to protect yourself and your children.

An extreme but very real possibility is that of "going underground." You would be amazed at the number of women and children living underground in this country. They have changed their looks and their identities as last resorts against relentless abusers who stalk them and threaten to kill them. For these women and children, the underground is the only hope of survival. If you need to investigate this option, contact the battered women's shelter in your community or one of the national sources listed in appendix B of this book, such as NOVA or Project Protect. Don't mince words when you talk to the counselor or advocate. If your life is in danger and you need protection, tell them so. If the shelter or program you contact doesn't provide that kind of protection, ask them to put you in touch with one that does.

A Word about Weapons

The easiest, smartest, and all-around best word about weapons is *don't*.

This book is about nonviolence. I do not advocate violence in any way, shape, or form *ever* to solve any kind of problem. My first recommendation to a woman who fears a life-threatening attack from her former partner is to move as far away from him as she possibly can and to go underground if necessary. Other recommendations include following all the safety information provided in this book as well as other publications containing information about personal safety; carrying a cellular telephone at all times; carrying a canister of pepper spray and a flashlight; and carrying a personal security alarm and a whistle.

The purchase of a weapon of any kind is a very personal decision. The most serious considerations are obeying the laws of your state and making certain beyond any shadow of a doubt that children have no access to the weapon. If you decide to make such a purchase, learn to use it and store it properly and safely. Take instruction from a professional. Too many women have been killed by the very weapons they purchased for protection.

If you find yourself facing criminal charges for any action you have taken against your abuser, contact the National Clearinghouse for the Defense of Battered Women in addition to your local legal advocacy group and battered women's program (information on all of these is in appendix B).

Restraining Orders and Orders of Protection

Time magazine reported in its 4 July 1994 issue:

> Disturbingly, the very pieces of paper designed to protect women—divorce decrees, arrest warrants, court orders of protection—are often read by enraged men as a license to kill. . . . That slip of paper, which documents his loss, may be interpreted by the man as a threat to his own life. "In a last-ditch, nihilistic act," says Roland Maiuro, director of Seattle's Harborview Anger Management and Domestic Violence Program, "he will engage in behavior that threatens the source of that threat." And in

the expanding range of rage, victims can include children, a woman's lawyer, the judge who issues the restraining order, the cop who comes between. Anyone in the way.

Know that abusers routinely violate restraining orders, orders of protection, no contact orders, emergency protective orders, orders of every kind. Sometimes they become more enraged because the order says that they have now been told by a judge that they can't have the one thing they want!

Quite often such orders are effective, though. As soon as you have any indication that your abuser is not going to leave you alone once you have left the relationship, you should request an order requiring your abuser to stay away from you and not to contact you. The methods of obtaining these orders and the exact names of the orders differ from one jurisdiction to another, so contact the battered women's program in your area or call the magistrate's office or the police department to request information on obtaining such an order. File a violation (report it to the police and the court) *every time your abuser violates the order.* Make a note of every phone call or attempted contact. This is the "paper trail" that may eventually lead him to jail if the harassment and/or stalking behaviors do not stop.

Be sure you are far away when he is served with the order. Give copies to the children's school teachers and principals, childcare workers, your boss, the security guard where you work, and anyone else who needs to know. Keep a copy of it with you at all times.

If You Have to Go to Court

If you bring charges against your abuser, if your state or city brings charges against him for his abuse of you and you are called as a witness, if you face criminal charges, if you find yourself in court testifying against him for the purposes of obtaining a divorce from him, or for any other reason, the following information may help you when you are faced with the unnerving ordeal of sitting in the witness chair. Be prepared for your abuser to present his case in one or more of the following ways:

He may try to convince the court

• that you exaggerate everything, that none of the incidents were as bad as you say;

• that you bruise easily, that you were out of control, and he had to restrain you in order to calm you down;

• that he has tried to keep the family together and that he is the real victim;

• that the family has had a few problems, but there has been no violence; or

• that you are the abusive one. He may even file charges against you to get even, and he may make anonymous calls to a child abuse hotline to report that you are neglecting or abusing your children.

He may try to convince you

• that he has friends in high places within the court system and that you would be wise to drop any charges you have brought against him because you cannot possibly succeed;

• that the case has been continued or the hearing has been postponed in an attempt to trick you into failing to appear; or

• that he knows the legal system and how to use it. He may use legal terms which you don't understand and otherwise try to intimidate and confuse you. He may make use of delaying tactics such as requests for continuances and changes of legal representation because such delays prolong his contact with you and also because they create financial hardship for you.

Keep Your Cool

The courts in this country will have come a long way when battered women are permitted to give their testimony away from the presence of their abusers. Any victim of domestic violence is terrified of her abuser, and knowing he may very well walk away from the courthouse that day and come straight to her door will almost certainly intimidate her into holding back important information. A child is allowed to speak to judges in chambers for the purpose of protecting that child. Battered women deserve and require that same protection. Ask your attorney if such a request can be made of the court.

The Centre County (Pennsylvania) District Attorney's Office has published the following suggestions for testifying in court. If you study them ahead of time, you will feel better prepared to present your testimony.

- Dress neatly.
- Be prepared by reviewing the facts of your testimony in your mind.
- Avoid distracting mannerisms.
- Be serious in the courtroom.
- Listen carefully to all questions.
- Wait for objections and do not answer until the judge has ruled.
- Take your time to think about each question before answering.
- Speak clearly and loudly.
- Do not volunteer information.
- Explain your answer if it cannot be answered truthfully and completely with a yes or no answer.
- Do not guess.
- Do not give your opinion unless asked to do so.
- Remain calm and courteous.

- You must answer all questions.
- Freely admit your conversations with all others about the case.
- Be yourself and try not to be nervous.
- Don't be afraid to cry.
- Avoid jurors during recess.
- Do not discuss your testimony with other witnesses.
- Above all, tell the truth.

The healthy and strong individual is the one who asks for help when he needs it. Whether he's got an abscess on his knee or in his soul.

—Rona Barrett

To keep our faces toward change and behave like free spirits in the presence of fate is strength undefeatable.

—Helen Keller

Prayer of St. Francis of Assisi

Lord, make me an instrument of Thy Peace.
Where there is hatred, let me sow love.
Where there is injury, pardon.
Where there is doubt, faith.
Where there is despair, hope.
Where there is darkness, light.
Where there is sadness, joy.
O Divine Master, grant that I may not so much seek to be consoled as to console; to be understood, as to understand; to be loved, as to love; for it is in giving that we receive, it is in pardoning that we are pardoned, and it is in dying that we are born to Eternal Life.

It's never too late to have a happy childhood.

—Seen on a button

Keep an open mind, but not so open that your brains fall out.

—Gilbert E. Allison
(my grandfather)

Chapter Eight

Getting Your Sanity Back

What Is Normal?

Sanity and *normal* are words we laypeople bandy about a lot, probably without having any real idea of what they mean. Immense textbooks filled with impressive theories, charts and graphs, and other clinical information have been published so that psychologists, psychiatrists, therapists, clinical social workers, and all the other counseling professionals can understand what sane and normal are so they will know when one of us is not.

But, this book is not for professionals. It is for ordinary women like you and me who have our own simple definitions of sanity and normality and want to know how to achieve some degree of both in our lives.

The two are intertwined in my mind. My definition of sanity/normality is being able to go to bed at night, fall asleep, and sleep soundly without waking up over and over again because of terrifying nightmares and "funny noises." It is being able to eat a meal without it coming back up or giving me stomach cramps if it stays down. It is being able to use my hands for whatever I need them for because they don't shake anymore. It is being able to think and study and concentrate.

It means feeling like I'm pretty much like every-body else and being free to live that way. It means working and learning and playing and dreaming. It means enjoying my family, enjoying my friends, and enjoying solitude. Most of all, it means looking into the future and seeing only exciting possibilities. San-ity/normality is, to me, freedom from fear of all kinds, but mostly freedom from the fear of being hurt.

Your definition may be slightly different or sub-stantially different, and that's fine, but the following suggestions will help you begin to achieve the sanity/normality your life probably has been missing for some time, however you define it.

Crying

I spent a lifetime with people telling me not to cry, and I learned to either not cry or stop crying in order to prevent further pain. I got so good at it that I was unable to cry at times when others expected me to cry, giving me a much undeserved reputation for stoicism with those who did not know me well.

On the other hand, sometimes I cried easily at times others thought inappropriate or embarrassing, giving me a reputation for being too sensitive and overly sentimental. I decided not to let that one bother me. It is still a struggle for me not to cry when I'm angry or embarrassed (sometimes I win the struggle, and sometimes I lose; *c'est la vie*) and I still cry at parades when the flag goes by, when I see a new baby for the first time, when I hear any version of "Amazing Grace," and every time Rhett leaves Scarlett. There are far worse things than being too sensitive or overly sentimental.

The point is that my crying mechanism was all messed up from years of being told not to cry or to stop crying. It has taken many years of introspection, many hours of counsel from good friends, and some

reading and research to arrive at one very simple conclusion: tears are normal and healthy, therefore you
should cry whenever you feel like it, and for as long as
you need to.

According to research conducted by Dr. William
H. Fry II (director of psychiatry at the Research Labo-
ratory of the Ramsey Clinic in St. Paul), Dr. Margaret
T. Crepeau of the University of Pittsburgh and others,
emotional tears are chemically different from tears
caused by irritants in the eye. Emotional tears contain
a greater concentration of protein and larger quanti-
ties of substances the body manufactures under stressful conditions. This may explain why we feel better
after a good cry, and why those who have better atti-
tudes about crying appear to be less likely to succumb
to stress-related illnesses.

What is so great about this information is that now
when someone tells you "crying doesn't help," you can
tell them scientific research proves it does. Part of you
knew that, didn't it?

What you are going through is tough. Very tough.
You are grieving the loss of a significant person in
your life even though you have accepted the fact that
he is abusive and even though you know you must
begin your life over again without him. You may still
love him; don't let anyone tell you that's not O.K. or
normal. Regardless of how bad your life with him was,
your grief for what was and for what might have been
is no less valid.

Give yourself time to grieve and, if that grief includes tears, let 'em fall. Think of every crying jag as
an emotional cleansing, a purgative for the spirit. If
someone pats you on the shoulder and says, "There,
there, don't cry" or worse, "Stop feeling sorry for yourself," remove yourself from that person's company as
quickly as possible and get on with your crying. On the
other hand, if you have a friend who knows how to be

there in the truest sense of the word, who will hold you while you cry and maybe even cry with you, count yourself fortunate indeed.

Of course, it is important to be aware of the effects our grieving may have on others, especially our children. Children need to know that it's O.K. to cry when something hurts, and you need to help them deal with their own anger and confusion during this time. There is nothing wrong with letting our children see our own tears and telling them that we hurt, too, and that we miss Daddy, but witnessing an adult's powerful grief can terrify a child.

Ask a family member or trusted friend to keep your children for a day or two so you can be alone, or try some other way to find a place and time for solitude when you feel your emotions becoming overwhelming. My favorite place to cry long and hard after leaving my abuser was in the shower after the boys were asleep. The noise of the water muffled the noise from me so the boys got a good night's sleep and I got to have the good cry I needed. A friend of mine whose husband died very young and quite suddenly asked some friends who owned a beach cottage if she could borrow it for the weekend. She didn't want her grieving to frighten her young daughter. Her mother kept the toddler, and my friend spent three days at a remote spot where she could shout, sob, cry, rage, pray, and throw things (at the water) in her anger and grief without hurting or scaring anyone. She spent the worst part of her anguish during those few days which enabled her to move forward in her grief and help her daughter deal with hers.

The key, then, is constructive grieving. Experts advise us to move toward grief, never away from it. Once you encounter it, move through it. Experience it fully. Let the sobs come up from way down inside you where it hurts. Beat the bed with a tennis racket. Throw rocks at the water. Talk to God. Tell Him you're angry. Tell Him you hurt and tell Him where it hurts. Don't pull back. Get it out. Don't let anyone tell you that "crying doesn't help." You know better. It does help.

You need to be aware, however, that uncontrollable crying over a long period of time may be a sign that you need to talk to a professional who specializes in grief issues. If you find you cannot work, care for your children, or attend to other responsibilities because you can't stop crying, talk to a counselor at the battered women's shelter, your clergyman, or someone else trained to help you determine whether you need to seek further counseling.

During the period of early recovery from your abusive past, you may also experience shock, numbness, confusion and disorganization, panic, nervousness, fear, anger, guilt, sadness, and emptiness. You may experience physiological signs of stress like sleeplessness, fatigue and lack of appetite, and symptoms such as an upset stomach or headache. If these symptoms last more than a few weeks, are particularly worrisome to you and/or do not respond to the usual over-the-counter remedies you use and the suggestions which follow here, do make an appointment with your family doctor or at the local health clinic.

Nurture Yourself

Nurturing means feeding something to promote its healthy growth and development. You haven't been nurtured for a long time. You may never have been nurtured. That doesn't matter; as the saying goes, that was then and this is now. You can nurture yourself, and I'm going to tell you how.

First of all, do a little nurture inventory. Make a list of ten things you like to do. Items on your list could be as simple as taking a long, relaxing bath or

spending an afternoon with a good book, or they could
be a little more adventuresome like hiking in the mountains or wave-riding in the ocean. No one will see the
list but you, so write down anything you want as long
as it is something *you* like to do. Don't let anyone else's
preferences—including the children's—influence your
list.

Now, look at your list and ask yourself how many
of those things you have done in the last six months to
a year. My guess is you haven't done very many of
them very often. You may be surprised to realize you
haven't done any of them in years.

You need to nurture yourself in four ways: physically, emotionally, mentally, and spiritually.

Physical Nurturing

To nurture yourself physically, you need to take
care of your body. Your body is a miraculous machine
that you probably never even think about. It is easy to
take your body for granted because it works so well,
but if you haven't taken good care of it in the past and
don't start taking care of it now, the stress you are
under will take its toll. Maybe not today or tomorrow,
or even in the next year, but before you know it, you
may find yourself with an ulcer, heart disease, or some
other stress-related illness or condition.

Make every effort to give up the things you do to
your body that actually damage it. This means smok-
ing, drinking, and using illegal drugs. I smoked for
more than twenty years. No one ever loved her ciga-
rettes more than I did. I resolved to quit when I saw
the anguish on my mother's face when my brother
died; I knew I did not want to be the cause of her ever
experiencing that kind of pain again if I could help it.
It took a few false starts and the help of my family
doctor (I used nicotine patches, for which you must
have a prescription), but I did it. So can you.

I've never been much of a drinker, nor used illegal drugs, but I have close friends and family members who have waged their own battles with alcohol and other substances. The ones who won their battles are the ones who turned to Alcoholics Anonymous, Narcotics Anonymous and other reputable self-help organizations, as well as treatment facilities. They all have told me that the decision to move toward sobriety is the single most important step they have ever taken in their lives because it saved their lives.

If you have a problem with alcohol or other substances, look in the yellow pages of your phone book under "Alcoholism-Information and Treatment Centers" or "Drug Abuse and Addiction-Information and Treatment." The phone numbers for Alcoholics Anonymous (AA) and Narcotics Anonymous (NA) will be there. If for some reason you can't find the number you need, call the information operator and get it. AA (or NA) will come to you if you ask them to, and they won't ask for a penny. All they want is to share with you the gift of sobriety if you are willing to accept it. If you are in need of additional services, they can help put you in touch with the people who can provide them. Always remember that the people in AA and NA have all been where you are; it's the only membership requirement. They understand what you are experiencing because they've been there. Give these good people a chance to show you what they have to offer.

You need to do other positive things for your body, and eating right is one of the most important. Stress causes some people to lose their appetites and causes others to overindulge. Listen to your body, and it will tell you what it needs. Give it nourishing food (whole grains and cereals, fruits and vegetables, dried beans and peas, nonfat dairy products, meats and fats in limited amounts) most of the time, and enjoy your favorite junk foods every now and then. Drink lots of water.

Your body also needs rest. Give it seven to eight hours of sleep every night. If you feel restless or have trouble falling asleep, drink warm milk (no hot chocolate; the caffeine will add to your problem) or herbal tea. Take a warm—not hot—bath. Practice total body relaxation (concentrate on relaxing each part of your body from your head to your toes, one section at a time) and slow, deep breathing. Count sheep. These time-honored home remedies really do work.

And, finally, your body needs to move. Exercise is a wonderful outlet for stress because it helps reduce anxiety and nervous tension. It also stimulates the release of endorphins, (our bodies' natural tranquilizers) making people who are active less inclined to stress-related depression.

You don't need to have access to a health club or gymnasium, and you don't need to sign up and pay for a class. Exercise is free and available to everyone. Take a walk. Take a hike. Do the jumping jacks and sit-ups you remember from high school (only don't cheat on the count this time). Play on the jungle gym at the playground—with or without children. Climb a tree. Run. Turn on the radio and dance. Like the ad says, just do it. Do it until your heart is beating faster than usual and you're sweating a little. Once you reach that level of exertion, stay there for twenty or thirty minutes. If you overdo it, your body will tell you; then you slow down. Don't worry. Have fun. (Of course, it's always a good idea to check with your doctor before starting any exercise program.)

You may think these suggestions rather too simplistic to be very effective, and indeed they will be for some people. Most of them are common sense, mama-always-told-you ways of taking care of yourself, but these are the very things we stop doing when we are stressed out, as women who are in abusive relationships or who have just left them are. Please see your family doctor or make an appointment at the local health clinic if you cannot sleep, if you sleep too much, if you are unable to eat at all or if eating makes you feel ill, or if you have a general sense of not being well.

Emotional Nurturing—Tell Your Story

Telling your story (talking about what you've been through) to someone you trust is one of the most effective ways to work through grief and all the accompanying stress. It is important that the person you share your story with be wholly supportive of you and nonjudgmental. If you don't have a close friend or family member who fits that description, the next paragraph may lead you to some of the best friends you will ever have.

Most women who have been abused find they are most comfortable talking with other women who have been abused. They understand each other and believe in each other like no one else can. The best place to find someone like that is by calling your local battered women's program and telling them you need to talk to a counselor one-on-one and also that you would like to be put in touch with a battered women's support group.

Former Surgeon General C. Everett Koop said, "I believe in self-help as an effective way of dealing with problems, stress, hardship and pain. . . . Mending people, curing them, is no longer enough; it is only part of the total health care that most people require." I have seen people who responded to nothing else respond to the nurturing and supportive atmosphere at a support group meeting, and I have seen healing no one had believed would or could occur.

If no such program or group exists in your area, that doesn't mean there are no other abused women in your area. Take my word for it—there are! Consider starting a group. Write or call the National Self-Help Clearinghouse, 33 West 42nd Street, New York, NY

10036, (212)642-2944. Request the brochure entitled *How To Start A Self-Help Support Group*.

If you feel the need to talk to someone one-on-one and no battered women's program exists in your area, call your local mental health association or the nearest hospital and ask to be put in touch with a counselor who specializes in the treatment of victims of domestic violence. Be specific about your needs because many counselors are not trained in and have no experience in this area. You wouldn't want your dentist to set your broken leg; likewise, you don't want a substance abuse counselor telling you how to recover from partner abuse.

You may choose to tell your story in other ways. Many victims of domestic violence have found creative outlets for their experiences. Writing in your diary, writing a poem, song, or story about your experiences can be extremely cathartic. You may want to tell your story in a drawing or painting or sculpture or photography. You may create music or dance to tell your story. If you have never experienced the satisfaction of creating something from an experience, I urge you to give it a try. You don't need lessons or expensive equipment. Opt for doing what comes naturally or, if you want some instruction, check out "teach yourself to . . ." books at the library. Stick with the basics as far as supplies go: paper and pencil, crayons, inexpensive paint sets and brushes, and clay, and that camera that's been on the top shelf of the closet forever. Some very impressive works of art have been created from the most humble materials and equipment.

In addition to telling your story in one fashion or another (ideally several), you need to do something you probably haven't done since you were a child: *play*. That's right, play. As adults, most of us have forgotten how to play. We have forgotten how to have so much fun that we lose all sense of time. We have forgotten the power of wonder that came so naturally to us as children. Remembering, relearning, and rehearsing how to play is a wonderful stress reliever and is a great way to get back in touch with your children and with yourself.

If you don't know where to start, choose something from this list of suggestions. Before you know it, you'll think of more.

Twenty-five Free or Inexpensive Nurturing Things to Do by Yourself

1. Take a bubble bath.
2. Go to the library and check out a romance, mystery or other popular novel. Curl up and read straight through a rainy weekend.
3. Have breakfast in bed or sitting on the floor watching Saturday morning cartoons.
4. Walk barefoot in the grass.
5. Write thank-you notes to people who have helped you or fan letters to people you admire.
6. Take up a hobby you can lose yourself in. Go to the library for books on how to get started. A lot of people have even established new careers by taking up a hobby or craft.
7. Paint your toenails.
8. Write a letter to each of your children. Tell each one what makes him special and how much you love him. Put the letters on their pillows when they're sleeping.
9. Plant a flower garden.
10. Interview friends or family members who are in their golden years. Ask them for advice on living a happy life. Write down what they say. Make a scrapbook with their photographs and advice.
11. Count your blessings.
12. Get a pen pal.

13. Enjoy some comfort food that reminds you of a happy time in your life. My comfort foods are oatmeal (like my mother made for me on cold mornings) and fudge cake (like my grandmother made when I came to visit).

14. Spend a day thinking and seeing like a child. Color in a coloring book or cut out paper dolls. Play jacks or marbles. (This is a suggestion probably best enjoyed on your day off. Your boss might not approve of you playing with your inner child on company time.)

15. Put a bird feeder or bird bath near your kitchen window. Watch and learn.

16. Dance.

17. Window shop.

18. Daydream.

19. Look in the newspaper for a list of "Things to do," usually published on or just before each weekend. Take advantage of freebies like lectures and sidewalk art shows.

20. Talk to God. Then listen.

21. Rent videos no one wants to see but you. Classic Bette Davis? Fred Astaire and Ginger Rogers? *The Creature from the Black Lagoon?* Whatever your taste, pick something *you* want to see. Make popcorn and curl up in your coziest pajamas or robe.

22. Explore your town. There are probably historical sights, parks, monuments, nature trails, and museums you've never seen.

23. Linger in bed on your day off. Sip a second cup of coffee and read the paper.

24. Go to the make-up counter at a fancy department store and request a makeover. Don't let the saleswoman talk you into buying anything you don't want or can't afford.

25. Test drive a luxury car.

Twenty-five Free or Inexpensive Nurturing Things to Do with the Kids

1. Have a picnic. Nothing fancy. Peanut butter and jelly sandwiches, some fruit, and a thermos of milk make the best picnics. Rainy-day picnics on a blanket on the floor of the living room are fun, too.

2. Tell elephant jokes and knock-knock jokes. If you can't remember any, there are books of them at the library. Really!

3. Use nature's playthings. Make mud pies. Fling yourselves into piles of autumn leaves. Make angels in the snow. Walk barefoot in wet grass. Catch raindrops and snowflakes on your tongue.

4. "Rain dance" in a warm spring rain (not in a thunderstorm, please). Everybody puts on their raincoats, grabs an umbrella, and heads outdoors to dance in the rain. Barefoot is even better.

5. Make funny faces and shadow pictures on the wall.

6. Talk to or write letters to God.

7. Build a "house" in the living room by draping a sheet or blanket over a card table. Pitch a tent in the backyard. Camp out with the kids in the "house" or tent.

8. Lie on your backs and stare at the sky. Make cloud pictures in the daytime. Count the stars at night. Don't forget to make a wish.

9. Skip.

10. Ask each child to tell you all about himself as if you have never met. Listen and learn. Then tell each child, "One of the things I really like about you is . . ."

11. Make pizza. Let everyone choose a topping and put it on.

12. Ride a carousel.

13. Blow bubbles.

14. Make finger puppets with scraps of fabric, yarn, cardboard, tin foil, crayons, and paper.

15. Make masks from paper bags.

16. Go to the library.

17. Teach your children games you enjoyed as a child such as Hopscotch, Red Rover, Red Light, Green Light, and Tag.

18. Go to the beach or river, or explore a local park or nature trail.

19. Two words: Silly Putty.

20. Read children's books together. Tell made-up stories.

21. Have a spelling bee.

22. Play in a garden sprinkler.

23. Let the children be king or queen for a day on their birthdays or on other special occasions like baptism or first communion. Royalty gets to choose the menu and have other privileges you determine.

24. Fly a kite.

25. Roller skate.

Yet another suggestion for nurturing yourself emotionally is to avoid stress as much as possible. *Oh, right, you say, I'm supposed to avoid stress during the most stressful time of my life.*

It's not as impossible as it sounds. If you follow even a few of the suggestions above for nurturing yourself physically and emotionally, you will reduce your stress level. Other ways to reduce stress include practicing muscle relaxation and deep breathing; closing your eyes and listening to audiotapes of nature sounds like rain and waves; and getting away in any way you can whether it be for an afternoon at the lake, overnight at your parents', a weekend at a friend's or a week in the mountains. Plan on taking a real vacation as soon as you can afford it. Save for it. Dream about it.

And *laugh*. Laughter is one of the most powerful restoratives known. It relaxes our muscles, improves our circulation and respiration, restores our objectivity, heightens our sense of hope, and certainly makes us more attractive to ourselves and others. If you can't remember the last time you laughed, rent some funny videos, watch a silly sit-com on TV, ask your children to tell you the funniest joke they've ever heard, or give a piece of ribbon to a kitten. Think back to activities, movies, and other things that used to make you laugh and resolve to experience them again. Then do it.

Another way to reduce stress is to establish priorities. Decide what is most important to you each day. Make a list of those things you hope to accomplish in the order of their importance. Focus your attention and energy on the first few items on your list, and put the others on a list for another day without feeling guilty about it. Better to go to bed at night knowing you did an outstanding job on the report you had to submit to your boss and made your daughter's birthday an occasion to remember than to go to bed feeling you did less than your best on everything on your list because you tried to do everything on your list.

Perhaps the most important suggestion I can offer you for nurturing both your physical and emotional health is *avoid contact with your ex-partner*. Ginny NiCarthy said it best in her groundbreaking book *Getting Free* (NiCarthy, 175):

> Keep in mind that it's a short step from the dinner table to a few drinks together, and an even shorter step from these to the bedroom. The longest road on a destructive journey, as well as on a worthwhile one, begins with a single step. You probably won't go back to your ex-partner if you don't go to bed with him. You won't go to bed with him if you don't cook dinner or go out drinking with him. You won't be tempted to cook for him or drink with him if you don't listen to his troubles or promises. And you can't listen to him if you're not in touch with him.

Unfortunately, the courts have made this crucial recovery element incredibly difficult and sometimes impossible for women who have children with their former partners by ordering joint or shared custody, by granting to the abusive parent frequent visitation with the children, and by ordering the mother to communicate with her ex-partner frequently regarding everything about the children from their grades in school to a bump on the knee. If this is the case in your own struggle, keep fighting. If you have shared custody, fight for sole custody as long as your strength, determination, and finances hold out. As much as possible, avoid contact with him when your ex-partner picks the children up for a visit. Don't invite him into your home and don't go outside. Speak as little as possible and don't be drawn into a conversation.

In both cases (shared custody and sole custody with visitation), document all evidence of your ex-partner's abuse of the children after each contact with him. Document what your children tell you regarding his or anyone else's abusive treatment of them, photograph any visual evidence, and take any child with a bruise or other injury to a doctor or clinic nurse and have the injuries and the child's story documented. If the court has given you that stern order to give your ex-partner frequent updates regarding the children's schooling and health, send him copies of important papers, report cards, progress reports and the like through the mail. If Susie has a toothache or Johnny skins his knee, send your ex-partner a note in the mail. Do whatever you can within the law to avoid contact with him or, at the very least, minimize it.

You know that your ex-partner is the worst stressor in your life. Do everything you can legally do to keep him out of your life.

Sometimes, however, following all these suggestions as well as suggestions from well-meaning friends and relatives just isn't enough. If you find that you or your children are in need of additional emotional support, talk to your counselor at the battered women's program or shelter (you *have* talked to them by now, haven't you?), call your local mental health association (in the Yellow Pages under "Mental Health Services"), call a crisis hotline (found in the front of most telephone directories), or call a clergyman. Don't be afraid or embarrassed to ask for help. Some of the most emotionally strong and sturdy people I know *got* that way because they sought counseling at one time and because they continue to turn to their counselors whenever they feel the need.

Mental Nurturing

Right after I left my abuser, I felt like I had scrambled eggs for brains. I was confused and disorganized. I had trouble making the simplest decisions. I might stand in the aisle at the supermarket for ten minutes trying to choose a breakfast cereal for the boys. Once, I had my shopping cart full and was suddenly overwhelmed by exhaustion and confusion. I wasn't sure I could remember how to write a check when I got to the checkout counter. I left the basket in the middle of the store, walked out empty-handed, and went home.

Don't worry if you experience similar episodes. You're not crazy (no more than anyone else, anyway) and you're not going crazy. It's just going to take a little while to organize your thinking again. Doing as many of the things listed above—under physical and emotional nurturing—as you can will help you begin to think straight again. Those support groups for battered women are especially valuable because they enable you to interact with others in your situation and see that all these awful things you are experiencing are happening to others, too. Once you know you're not alone, you may even find that you're able to laugh at some of the crazy things you've done. I still smile when I remember finding my keys in the refrigerator. And the time I called my dentist's office to schedule a mammogram.

Besides talking to other victims of abuse and sharing your experiences with them, I urge you to read and study something. Anything that interests you. What have you always wished you knew more about? Stained glass? Filmmaking? The Great Depression? French cooking? Be your own teacher. Check out books about your subject at the library. Take notes from your reading and studying. When your curiosity about that subject has been satisfied, choose another one.

Do mental exercises such as math and logic problems. Work crossword puzzles and other word games. Put jigsaw puzzles together.

If you can afford to, take a class in something that interests you. If you can't afford to but really want to, go to the financial aid officials at the school where the course is offered. They will help you work something out in the way of a scholarship, loan, or work/study program. If the class you want to take but can't afford is at a community center or through a recreation department, speak to the person in charge. Be honest. Tell the person who can help you that you want to take the class but don't have the money. Offer to work in exchange for your tuition. Everybody respects a sincere desire to learn. If you project that sincere desire, someone will see to it that you get the chance.

Take time to read. The following suggestions and other books on similar topics can be found at most public libraries:

1. *The Power of Positive Thinking* by Dr. Norman Vincent Peale

2. *When Bad Things Happen to Good People* by Harold S. Kushner

3. *Why Me? Coping With Grief, Loss and Change* by Pesach Krauss and Morrie Goldfischer

4. *The Language of Letting Go* by Melody Beattie

5. *Care of the Soul* by Thomas Moore

6. *When Anger Hurts* by Matthew McKay, Ph.D., Peter Rogers, Ph.D., and Judith McKay, R.N.

7. *How to Find Your Mission in Life* by Richard N. Bolles

8. *Happy People: What Happiness Is, Who Has It, and Why* by Jonathan Freedman

9. *Never Alone: A Personal Way to God* by Joseph F. Girzone

10. The Bible

These are some of my personal favorites. Explore your library shelves and find others.

Spiritual Nurturing

If you are like I was when I lived with abuse, you probably haven't nurtured your spirit in years. We nurture our spirits by spending quiet time alone. We use the time to reflect on our lives and our experiences, what they mean and what we are learning along the way of this incredible journey. We recall the religious teachings and traditions of our families and explore our deepest beliefs about God. We pray. We come to Him with the innocence and openness of children and ask for comfort and guidance. Spend quiet time talking to God.

Talk to your children about God. Teach them to pay attention to and appreciate His handiwork: tell them to look up at an incredible sunset or a rainbow, let them watch the cat give birth to and nurse her kittens, explain how the rain and the sun make the flowers and trees and fruits and vegetables grow, and show them how family members are supposed to love and care for one another. Make sure they know that God is present in all things and in all areas of their lives.

Then remind yourself of these things.

I like living. I have sometimes been wildly, despairingly, acutely miserable, racked with sorrow, but through it all I still know quite certainly that just to be alive is a grand thing.

—Agatha Christie

Comes the Dawn
(poet unknown)

After a while you learn the subtle difference
Between holding a hand and chaining a soul,
And you learn that love doesn't mean leaning
And company doesn't mean security,
And you begin to learn that kisses aren't contracts
And presents aren't promises,
And you begin to accept your defeats
With your head up and your eyes open
With the grace of a woman, not the grief of a child,
And you learn to build all your roads on today
Because tomorrow's ground is too uncertain for plans
And futures have a way of falling down in mid-flight.
After a while you learn
That even sunshine burns if you get too much.
So you plant your own garden and decorate your own soul
Instead of waiting for someone to bring you flowers.
And you learn that you really can endure,
That you really are strong,
And you really do have worth,
And you learn and learn.
With every good-bye you learn.

The way I see it, if you want the rainbow, you gotta put up with the rain.

—Dolly Parton

Courage is the price that life exacts for granting peace.

—Amelia Earhart

Chapter Nine

Starting Over

Life Lessons

Putting your abusive past behind you isn't easy. In fact, it's hard work, but there are some specific techniques you can practice that will make it easier.

One of the most positive ways of letting go of negative experiences is to view them as just that—experiences. They were life lessons. Life lessons can help us grow and become better, stronger people—if we let them. They can also make us bitter and hard if we let them. Find quiet time to reflect on your abusive relationship without judging or thinking about what you could have or should have done. Be as objective as you can (of course you can't be completely) and ask yourself what you have learned from the relationship. What did you learn about your partner? What did you learn about yourself? What did you learn about what you don't want in a relationship? What did you learn about what you do want in a relationship? Write your answers down in the form of positive statements. For example, "I have learned that I am stronger than I thought I was" and "I have learned that I want to be respected in a relationship." Power over a painful past is gained by learning from the experiences it provided. Use the past for insight.

What about Forgiveness?

You may have been told by others that in order to let go of the past, you must forgive the person who hurt you. I'm uncomfortable with the word *forgive* when speaking of abuse because some women interpret forgiveness as something they should do for their abusers. They then become caught up in a cycle of trying to forgive and being frustrated because they find they just can't. So much damage has been done to their bodies, their minds, their hearts, their spirits, and in many cases, their children, that forgiving the person who wreaked all of that destruction is impossible. When others continue to tell the victims they must forgive their abusers in order to get on with their lives, the victims feel as if they are failing at something vitally important, yet another blow to their already fragile self-images.

Also, when told how important it is to forgive their abusers, most abused women remember where such forgiveness got them in the past. For these women, forgiveness implies being submissive once again, which, in turn, opens them up to potential injury again. After all, they say, didn't we forgive our abusers time and time again? And, didn't they promise over and over that, if we would just forgive them, the abuse would never happen again? And, weren't we abused time and time again?

Besides, one would have to be a martyr to keep forgiving someone who is still causing her anguish as many abusers do long after their ability to physically or even verbally batter us is gone. Child custody suits, nuisance suits over petty matters, drawn-out child support negotiations, anonymous child abuse tips phoned in to hotlines—these are just some of the ways abusers continue to emotionally batter their ex-partners for as long as they are able. Others go even further, stalking their partners day and night, threatening to hurt or kill them, their children and other family members, and exhibiting other frightening behaviors. By definition, being a martyr is not a healthy way to spend one's time, so I'm not going to tell you that you need to find it in yourself to forgive him.

Instead, I will tell you that you need to do only what the law requires you to do where he is concerned, and save your forgiveness for yourself.

I can hear the outcry from some therapists, clergy, and other counselors already. "Don't tell her to forgive herself! That implies she's done something wrong or that she is somehow to blame for the abuse! She didn't cause the abuse, and she has nothing to forgive herself for!"

Of course, all of that is absolutely true. You haven't done anything wrong and you are not to blame in any way for the abuse you and your children have suffered. You truly do not have anything to forgive yourself for. The point I'm trying to make, though, is that many of us *feel* as if we didn't "get it" soon enough, we feel that we are at fault for not leaving sooner or for leaving and coming back again and again, and we feel that maybe, just maybe, if we had tried one more time or one more idea, we might have been able to make our abusers stop abusing us. In many cases, we feel that we weren't good mothers because our children got hurt before we made the final decision to leave. Those feelings are the ones we have to put behind us, and for some of us, forgiving ourselves is the only way to do that. Let me show you what I mean.

After I left my abusive marriage, several well-meaning friends and relations told me that, in order to get on with my life and let go of my past, I had to forgive the two men who had hurt me so badly. Well, I tried. After all, it sure sounded like good advice.

The harder I tried to forgive them, though, the more they inched their ways back into my life. If I am truly forgiving, I reasoned, then I will speak to them politely, agree with them that what's past is past and no longer matters, and by so doing I will begin to feel better and better about myself because I will be free of the hostility I am carrying around.

Wrong. It didn't work that way at all. Each time I spoke politely to one of them, he took it as friendliness. If I agreed that what was past was past and no longer mattered, he took that to mean what was past was okay and it would be okay if it happened again. I only felt worse and worse, more and more like a victim, more and more caught up in a cycle that seemed to have no escape. Instead of feeling less hostile, my hostility grew horns.

My forgiveness was misdirected, and I was sending the wrong signals to my abusers. I had not established boundaries. My southern upbringing had made it extremely difficult for me to be rude to anyone, even these two men. Southern tradition dictates to little girls that they put themselves last, that they see to it that others around them are comfortable, and that they are never rude to anyone, no matter how badly that person is behaving. Southern traditions are lovely, but they do not teach little girls to set boundaries and take care of themselves.

I had to learn to hang up the phone when one of my abusers used telephone conversations to begin his abuse again. I had to learn that no one—*no one*—has the right to belittle, mock and/or humiliate me and that, if they try, *I have the right to hang up the phone.* If they try to do it face-to-face with me, *I have the right to remove myself from that person's presence.* I had to learn that there was nothing in my final divorce decree that said I had to listen to my ex-partner verbally abuse me. Protecting yourself is not rude; it is the wise and loving thing to do for yourself.

If you find that your attempts to forgive your abuser are only resulting in further abuse, examine the subtle signals you may be sending. Ask a battered women's counselor what your forgiveness may be implying to your abuser and to give you some suggestions on how you might better relate to your former partner if the law requires you to because of child custody/visitation issues. If no children are involved, you are not required to have any contact with your abuser and you need to practice not having contact with him until you are able to break from him completely. Each time you hang up on him, it will be easier to hang up the next time. Each time you walk away from him or refuse to see him, it will be easier to avoid that kind of contact in the future. Remember that establishing boundaries to protect yourself takes practice. You are unlearning years of learned responses. Give yourself time to learn new ones. Then practice them.

This is where forgiving yourself comes in. Like I did, you may find yourself repeating in your own mind all the put-downs and insults your abuser heaped on you in the past: "How could I be so stupid?" "What, letting him abuse me once wasn't enough? I had to let him do it again?" "What is wrong with me that I keep repeating this cycle?" I spent several years letting those old tapes play over and over again in my head. I blamed myself for everything that went wrong. I didn't need an abuser; I was beating *myself* up!

Then, one day, a good friend of mine said to me, "You did the best you could at the time and under very difficult circumstances." Those were the most comforting words I had ever heard. I had done the best I could at the time—and under very difficult circumstances. Maybe I hadn't handled everything the way someone else might have, and maybe I hadn't done things the way I would do them if I had them to do over again, but I had done the very best I could at the time.

I had survived the abuse, and I had survived my mistakes and the mistakes of others, and I was learning more every day about standing on my own two feet and being responsible for myself and my children. That was really all that mattered, so I forgave myself by telling myself that those mistakes were really just more life lessons. I had learned from them important things about myself and others and the way the world works (which, by the way, is not only not always fair, but is often unfair) that I could not have learned any other way. I began to feel rather proud. I had come a long way, and it had been a hard way. And, I was still standing. I figured that was worth forgiving myself anything and everything.

Do this for yourself. Resolve today to stop beating yourself up. If you've made mistakes, well, welcome to the human race. Learn from them and then let 'em go. Don't become your own abuser. Be very, very gentle with yourself.

Trust

You may find you are all but unable to trust anyone for a time. You may find yourself thinking everyone has an ulterior motive or a hidden agenda and that their intent is to take advantage of or hurt you in some way. You may even find yourself (as I did) flinching when someone reaches toward you, even if their intent is to hug you or just put an arm around your shoulders. You have learned to keep your guard up, to protect yourself and your children, to watch other people for signs of potential violence. You are used to being ever-vigilant. Know that that's okay for right now, but know how to deal with it.

The smartest and safest thing you can do while you are in the very early stages of recovery is to limit your contacts and conversations to those you know you can

trust, those who love you and want to help you recover. This includes family members and close friends
(if they are supportive of you and your decisions and
not if they are friends of your ex-partner and hope to
get the two of you together again), clergy and other
professional counselors, and especially the contacts I
hope you have made by this time with the staff and
other clients of your local battered women's program.

Now is *not* the time for going to clubs and other
places where singles gather to meet. Don't let well-
meaning friends try to fix you up with a date or drag
you along to parties and other large social functions
until and unless you know that your initial vulnerabil-
ity and insecurity are fading and until and unless you
are feeling strong and in control of your emotions
once again. It's a good idea to ask for help from a
battered women's counselor when trying to decide
whether you are ready to begin socializing and making
new friends again. When still in early recovery, you
will be tempted to say you are feeling strong and in
control again when you actually are not. Ask the opinion of someone who has a more objective view of you.

When you do begin to socialize and meet new
people once more, always remember that batterers can
be and often are extremely charming men. They know
all the right things to say; "I can't understand how a
man could ever hit a woman" and "He must be crazy
to let someone like you get away" are two popular
consoling comments. Those words are so flattering and
restorative to a battered woman's bruised and dimin-
ished ego. The good guys of the world will say the
same words and mean them, but it's how *some* men—
the bad guys—gain the control and power they use to
manipulate and eventually abuse their victims. At this
point in your life you are very vulnerable to falling
into a relationship with a charming man who could
turn out to be your next batterer. Because of your

history, certain aspects of his personality will feel familiar to you. Always remember that we are drawn to and attracted by people who feel familiar to us.

Ask the opinion of someone trained to spot the warning signs if you feel your perception is still a bit skewed.

"Heart"

During the early stages of your recovery from abuse, study the list of twenty-five behaviors that are seen in people who are abusive (chapter 4). Learn to spot potential abusers and avoid them. When a man's behavior makes you uncomfortable, forget the manners your mother taught you and tell him so. Then get away from him.

Study the following list, too. It is based on the highly successful Twelve Step Program developed by the founders of Alcoholics Anonymous.

Help End Abusive Relationship Tendencies
("HEART")
The Twelve Steps Toward Abuse-Free Relationships

1. Admit that we have been involved in an abusive situation and that we need the help and support of others.

2. Realize that we can only change and make choices for our own lives.

3. Believe that we must accept responsibility for our own feelings and behavior.

4. Acknowledge that we are valuable human beings and deserve dignity and respect.

5. Make a personal history of our lives to discover our strengths, weaknesses, and needs.

6. Share our personal history with another.

7. Make a decision to do the necessary work to change our lives and begin making healthy choices.

8. Develop support systems and resources which can aid in making these changes.

9. Realize that our happiness does not depend on a relationship but lies within ourselves.

10. Clear the air with friends and loved ones who may have been hurt by us while we were in the abusive relationship, unless this would be dangerous for ourselves or others.

11. Learn to distinguish between a healthy and an abusive relationship and continue to "take inventory" of ourselves and our relationships.

12. Having developed an awareness as a result of these steps, we share this knowledge with others and practice these steps in our own lives.

Patricia Evans (*The Verbally Abusive Relationship*) offers the following list of "Basic Rights in a Relationship." Teach them to your children, and insist on them yourself.

- The right to good will from the other.
- The right to emotional support.
- The right to be heard by the other and to be responded to with courtesy.
- The right to have your own view, even if your mate has a different view.
- The right to have your feelings and experience acknowledged as real.
- The right to receive a sincere apology for any jokes you find offensive.
- The right to clear and informative answers to questions that concern what is legitimately your business.
- The right to live free from accusation and blame.
- The right to live free from criticism and judgment.
- The right to have your work and your interests spoken of with respect.

- The right to encouragement.
- The right to live free from emotional and physical threat.
- The right to live free from angry outbursts and rage.
- The right to be called by no name that devalues you.
- The right to be respectfully asked rather than ordered.

Avoiding Distorted Thinking

Everyone falls victim to distorted thinking at one time or another, but women who have been in abusive situations are especially vulnerable because they have been told for so long that they are "crazy," "nuts," "emotionally disturbed," and so on. They have spent years not trusting their own judgment, being certain their perceptions are wrong, believing they can't make a valid decision and follow through on it.

Some examples of distorted thinking include the following:

1. Black and White Thinking—Everything is good or bad. You are either perfect or you are a failure. You see everything in terms of black and white and fail to see the many shades of gray.

2. Rule Making—You have a list of strict rules about how you and everyone else should act. You get angry when others break the rules, and you feel guilty when you break them.

3. Overgeneralizing—You base a conclusion on a single piece of evidence. If you have had a single bad experience, you expect that it will happen to you again and again.

4. Personalizing—Believing others are judging you all the time, that everything they say or do is in reaction to you. You also compare yourself to others and are always trying to decide who is smarter, prettier, etc.

5. Changing Others—You believe you can change others if you just put enough pressure on them or plead with them long enough. You feel the need to change someone because you believe your happiness lies in him.

These are just a few of the many ways in which our thinking can become distorted. When you find yourself sending negative messages to yourself about yourself, that is most certainly distorted thinking. You need to make a concerted effort to become aware of such thinking and practice new and positive ways of thinking. For example, when you think *Maybe if I color my hair, I will look prettier and people will like me more*, that is distorted thinking. But when you think *Maybe if I color my hair, I will feel more attractive and that will boost my spirits*, that is healthy thinking. When you think *I am so sick of Angie's leaving her coffee cup in the sink in the break room for someone else to wash. Her messiness is driving me up the wall*, that is distorted thinking. When you think *I'm not washing Angie's coffee cup for her anymore*, that is healthy thinking. And when you think *Every relationship I've ever had with a man was abusive. I'll never take a chance on love again*, that is distorted thinking. But, when you think *Every relationship I've ever had with a man was abusive. I'm going to start taking better care of myself and enjoying my life and my own company. If the possibility of another relationship comes into my life, I will remember and practice what I have learned about healthy relationships*, that is healthy thinking.

Will I Love Again?

Why are some women able to escape abusive relationships while others remain in them until they die? Some domestic violence experts cite the presence of a compassionate observer or helping witness in the abused woman's childhood as part of what gave some bit of hope to the women who escaped or otherwise enabled them to save themselves. This compassionate observer was a caring adult who positively influenced and touched the life of the woman when she was a child and living in an abusive home.

My grandfather was one of my compassionate observers; his influence was significant because he told me frequently that I was a great kid and because we had fun together. I was very fortunate in that there were other such compassionate observers in my life: my Aunt Charlsie, a strong, independent and chronically cheerful woman with a great sense of adventure who often whisked me away on wonderful trips to far-away places; and, of course, my own mother who, in spite of the abuse she suffered in her marriage to my father, always managed to make it very clear to my brother and me that she loved and cherished us. Along the way there were other relatives, teachers, parents of friends, and other adults who made contributions to undoing the damage and binding up my emotional wounds.

Take some time to remember who your own compassionate observers were. Remember what they said to you, what they did, or how they looked at you that let you know you were loved and important. Remembering when we were loved, who loved us, and what it felt like to be loved is what gives us the courage to seek real love again.

When I began working on this book, I had every intention of not talking about my second marriage or my mother's second marriage. The reason was that I didn't want readers to become preoccupied with finding a new relationship. The purpose of this book is to help each reader identify an abusive relationship, get out of it if she is in one, and recover from it once she is out.

But, everyone who was involved in this project insisted that I must tell what happened to my mother and to me after we were out of our abusive relationships. They insisted that these stories would let readers know that there is hope of finding real and lasting love, even though they agreed with me that the most important lessons are learning to be good to yourself, to find joy in your own company and counsel, to live a life free of violence and to teach your children the ways of nonviolence. That said, then, I will tell you about some very happy endings.

My mother suffered greatly for some time after my father left us. Her self-esteem was shattered and her heart broken. Coming as she did from "the old school," she had truly believed that if she just kept trying to do everything right (even though the rules of right changed from one day to the next with my father), my father would eventually stop abusing all of us and would stop having extramarital affairs. She was in a state of shock when everything she had been taught to believe in was proven wrong and her world crashed in around her.

Sometime later, my mother (a school teacher) was asked to meet with her principal after school one day. She assumed he wanted to talk to her about some classroom matter and was, in fact, a little nervous. Teachers get worried when summoned to the principal's office just like students do! But, what he told her was that a close friend of his, a widower, was joining him and his wife for dinner and they would like her to be their guest and the dinner partner of their friend. She agreed.

The man who came to dinner and my mother have been happily—no, make that ecstatically—married for twenty-four years. Theirs has always been a marriage of warmth, devotion, mutual respect, and admiration. They also have more fun on any given day than should be allowed by law. And, no one could have asked for a more wonderful stepfather than the one I have.

After my own abusive marriage ended, I also was invited to be a guest at a dinner party and the dinner partner of someone I had met once but hadn't seen in many years. When my blind date brought me home after the dinner party, my sides and face hurt from laughing so much. I honestly couldn't remember the last time I had laughed!

Over the next few months, I fell in love with this big, gentle man who enjoyed making me laugh. Our dates were simple, casual, and very inexpensive as neither of us had much money. We spent a lot of time playing with the children, doing the joyful family-type activities I had always wanted my children to experience and had always wanted to experience myself.

We have been happily—no, make that ecstatically—married for eleven years. He has raised my two boys as if they were his own. We have experienced numerous traumas during our marriage, but they were traumas brought on by circumstances and/or people outside of our marriage and/or beyond our control, not by mean or hurtful things we did to each other. We faced them together, as partners, as a team committed to the best possible solution for all concerned. We have faced terrible losses, and we have known much joy.

We discuss every decision until we reach some form of agreement or compromise, whether it be about wallpaper or a career move. Neither of us makes "power moves" against the other, and neither of us would ever intentionally say or do anything to hurt the other. We take enormous pride in one another's accomplishments, and each of us is the other's best friend. I always thought that "best friend" business was rather trite when I heard others say it about their marriages, but that was before I understood or experienced what a good marriage was.

We are different in many ways, but our differences complement each other. More important, we respect these differences and really listen to each other's opinions. Most important of all, we both are committed to these beliefs:

Love is consistent. It is the same today as yesterday, and it will be the same tomorrow.

Love does not hurt.

You may have realized by now that I could write an entire book about happy marriages (and, hey, I might do that), so I'll stop for now. Just know that happy endings do happen. I wish for every reader a safe, caring, loving relationship with another person at some point in the future, but I wish for you first and above all else safety in your own home and a loving relationship with yourself.

The Way of Nonviolence

Whether or not you someday choose to enter into a new relationship, you can begin learning the elements of a nonviolent relationship right now. If and when the possibility of a new relationship occurs and if you decide you want to investigate that possibility, these are the elements to keep in mind when determining whether your potential partner sees eye-to-eye with you on what constitutes a good relationship. (This list is based on the Equality Wheel which is used for instruction in many anger management courses).

1. Negotiation and fairness—seeking mutually satisfying solutions to conflict; accepting change; being willing to compromise.

2. Nonthreatening behavior—talking and acting so that both partners feel safe and comfortable expressing themselves and doing things.

3. Respect—listening to one another nonjudgmentally; being emotionally affirming and understanding; valuing each other's opinions.

4. Trust and support—supporting one another's goals in life; respecting each other's right to his or her own feelings, friends, activities, and opinions.

5. Honesty and accountability—accepting responsibility for self; admitting being wrong; communicating openly and truthfully.

6. Responsible parenting—sharing parental responsibilities; being a positive nonviolent role model for the children.

7. Shared responsibility—mutually agreeing on a fair distribution of work; making family decisions together.

8. Economic partnership—making money decisions together; making sure both partners benefit from financial arrangements.

Teach Your Children Well

Following are some important issues to discuss with your children. They are from an article by Pam Shea, a community education coordinator on domestic violence.

1. Teach your child ways to solve problems without using violence. Reinforce this message by your own actions—model problem solving and think twice about physical punishment.

2. Show your child that she/he is important. Children with good self-esteem are less likely to be abused or to become abusive.

3. Cut down on exposure to violent television shows (this includes cartoons), and when your child does watch something violent, talk about it during and after.

4. Opt for nonviolent toys and games. Instead, choose those that promote cooperation, problem solving, and caring.

5. Break away from outdated gender stereotypes—yes, it's O.K. for boys to show their feelings and it's O.K. for girls to be assertive.

6. Take every opportunity to show your child you love him/her. "Four hugs a day are necessary for survival, eight are good for maintenance, and twelve for growth." (Virginia Satir)

7. Teach your children that they have rights and model assertiveness. Help them learn to say no to things that scare them or make them uncomfortable.

8. Let your child know that she/he can come to you as an ally if she/he needs help. Believe and support your child if she/he does need help.

9. Respect your child. This teaches him/her to respect self and others.

Letting Go

Letting go means different things to different people. To the anxious parents sending their son or daughter off to college, letting go is a bittersweet combination of pride and sadness. The spouse of an alcoholic learns that letting go means continuing to care about the alcoholic, but not taking care of him anymore. And, the woman who is recovering from an abusive relationship learns that letting go means putting her painful past behind her and accepting that she cannot fix everything in her life that has been broken. Even more important, it means learning to recognize people who are potential abusers so that she doesn't repeat the same destructive patterns her life has followed thus far, *and* it means helping her children *un*learn what they have seen of family relationships and teaching them new ways to interact and negotiate with others.

In her book *The Language of Letting Go* (New York: Harper Collins Publishing [1990], 351), Melody Beattie says, "Letting go is the action part of faith." I love that—the action part of faith. So many times we say to ourselves, "I have faith in God. I believe in Him. I say my prayers. Why are things not working out for me?" Maybe it's because we haven't taken the action part of that faith, which is to let go.

Letting go is scary because it means giving up trying

to control everything—results, people, desires, needs, feelings, ideas, *everything*—releasing our grasp on these things so that we are open to receiving the gifts we are meant to have.

Says Beattie (ibid., 351),

> Letting go means we acknowledge that hanging on so tightly isn't helping to solve the problem, change the person, or get the outcome we desire. It isn't helping *us*. In fact, we learn that hanging on often blocks us from getting what we want and need. . . . There is magic in letting go. Sometimes we get what we want soon after we let go. Sometimes it takes longer. Sometimes the specific outcome we desire doesn't happen. Something better does . . . Letting go creates the optimum environment for the best possible outcomes and solutions.

I have a scrap of paper, torn from an old calendar, on the bulletin board over my desk. The scrap is printed with the following thought: "One of the exciting wonders of recognizing our need for control and beginning to let it go is the weightlessness of the anticipation that everything is possible. When we realize we don't know, we are open to what we don't know."

Remember that letting go is a process, not a one-time event. It will not happen overnight. Be patient.

Man's inhumanity to man makes countless thousands mourn.

—Robert Burns

We are confronted primarily with a moral issue. It is as old as the Scriptures and is as clear as the American Constitution.

—John F. Kennedy

Blessed are the peacemakers.

—Matthew 5:9

A Prayer for Children
by Ina J. Hughes

We pray for children who put chocolate fingers everywhere, who like to be tickled, who stomp in puddles and ruin their new pants, who sneak Popsicles before supper, who erase holes in math workbooks, who can never find their shoes.

And we pray for those who stare at photographers from behind barbed wire, who can't bound in the street in a new pair of sneakers, who never go to the circus, who live in an X-rated world.

We pray for children who bring us sticky kisses and fistfuls of dandelions, who sleep with the dog and bury the goldfish, who hug us in a hurry and forget their lunch money, who cover themselves with Band-Aids and sing off-key, who squeeze toothpaste all over the sink, who slurp their soup.

And we pray for those who never get dessert, who have no safe blanket to drag behind them, who watch their parents watch them die, who can't find any bread to steal, who don't have any rooms to clean up, whose pictures aren't on anybody's dresser, whose monsters are real.

We pray for children who spend all their allowance before Tuesday, who throw tantrums in the grocery store and pick at their food, who like ghost stories, who shove dirty clothes under the bed and never rinse the tub, who get visits from the tooth fairy, who don't like to be kissed in front of the carpool, who squirm in church and scream in the phone, whose tears we sometimes laugh at, and whose smiles can make us cry.

We pray for those whose nightmares come in the daytime, who will eat anything, who aren't spoiled by anybody, who go to bed hungry and cry themselves to sleep, and who live and move, but have no being.

We pray for children who want to be carried and for those who must, for those we never give up on and for those who don't get a second chance. For those we smother . . . and for those who will grab the hand of anybody kind enough to offer it.

Chapter Ten

When Someone You Care about Is Abused

For the Love of a Child

Child abuse is a real and pervasive evil found in virtually every country and culture in the world. In the United States alone, three out of ten children are abused and four thousand children die each year as the result of child abuse. These children often grow up to inflict the violence they endured on society in the form of violent crime. Also, child abuse almost always leads to violence in the next generation; those who were abused as children grow up to abuse their own children or enter into relationships with partners who will continue to abuse them and the children born into those relationships. At the very least, children who are abused carry with them into adulthood profound effects of that abuse, such as the inability to trust others, reluctance or inability to form lasting relationships, chronic depression, and other disorders.

Few situations create as much frustration and anger for a caring adult as the realization that a child they know is being abused. The adult may be a relative, a family friend, a neighbor, or just an acquaintance. Whatever the relationship to the child, the caring adult often feels helpless to do anything to help the abused child.

While school officials, medical personnel, and other professionals are required by law to report suspected cases of child abuse to the appropriate agencies, these individuals are also often frustrated and wish they could do more than simply file a report.

In every case, the caring adult who becomes aware that a child is being abused can help in some way, but often fails to because he or she is afraid of making a mistake, worried that an error in judgment could cause needless hardship for the family. It is certainly true that many reports of alleged child abuse have been proven invalid and have actually *created* trauma for the child and the child's family. And, as mentioned earlier in this book, many abusers make false allegations about their former partners to child abuse hotlines in an effort to get even. It is important to know what to look for and to be very sure of one's observations and conclusions.

The following signs of child abuse are from the *Interdisciplinary Glossary on Child Abuse and Neglect: Legal, Medical, Social Work Terms*, published by the Department of Health and Human Services.

Physical Abuse

Child's Appearance:

• Bruises and welts (on the face, lips or mouth; in various stages of healing; on large areas of the torso, back, buttocks, or thighs; in unusual patterns, clustered or reflective of the instrument used to inflict them; on several different surface areas)

• Burns (cigar or cigarette burns; glove or sock-like burns or doughnut-shaped burns on the buttocks or genitalia indicative of immersion in hot liquid; rope burns on the arms, legs, neck, or torso; patterned burns that show the shape of the item—iron, grill, etc.—used to inflict them)

- Fractures (skull, jaw, or nasal fractures; spiral fractures of the long arm and leg bones; fractures in various states of healing; multiple fractures; any fracture in a child under the age of two)
- Lacerations and abrasions (to the mouth, lips, gums or eyes; to the external genitalia)
- Human bite marks

Child's Behavior:

- Wary of physical contact with adults
- Apprehensive when other children cry
- Demonstrates extremes in behavior (e.g., extreme aggressiveness or withdrawal)
- Seems frightened of parents
- Reports injury by parents

Neglect

Child's Appearance:

- Consistently dirty, unwashed, hungry, or inappropriately dressed
- Without supervision for extended periods of time or when engaged in dangerous activities
- Constantly tired or listless
- Has unattended physical problems or lacks routine medical care
- Is exploited, overworked, or kept from attending school
- Has been abandoned

Child's Behavior:

- Is engaging in delinquent acts (e.g., vandalism, drinking, prostitution, drug use, etc.)
- Is begging or stealing food
- Rarely attends school

Sexual Abuse

Child's Appearance:

- Has torn, stained, or bloody underclothing
- Experiences pain or itching in the genital area
- Has bruises or bleeding in external genitalia, vagina, or anal regions
- Has venereal disease
- Has swollen or red cervix, vulva, or perineum
- Has semen around mouth or genitalia or on clothing
- Is pregnant

Child's Behavior:

- Appears withdrawn or engages in fantasy or infantile behavior
- Has poor peer relationships
- Is unwilling to participate in physical activities
- Is engaging in delinquent acts or runs away
- States he/she has been sexually assaulted by parent/caretaker

Emotional Maltreatment

Child's Appearance:

- Emotional maltreatment, often less tangible than other forms of child abuse and neglect, can be indicated by behaviors of the child and the caretaker.

Child's Behavior:

- Appears overly compliant, passive, undemanding
- Is extremely aggressive, demanding, or regal
- Shows overly adaptive behaviors, either inappropriately adult (e.g., parents other children) or inappropriately infantile (e.g., rocks constantly, sucks thumb, is enuretic), lags in physical, emotional, and intellectual development, attempts suicide

Anyone who believes he or she observes any of these signs of possible abuse in a child should realize that some of the characteristics listed above can be caused by illness or certain physical or environmental conditions. For example, a child who is enuretic (wets the bed) may have a urinary tract infection, congenital weakness in or deformity of the muscles that control bladder function, or any one of a number of other physical ailments. A child who starts sucking his thumb may simply have a new baby brother or sister at home and be longing for some extra attention. A child with a broken arm or a cut lip may have fallen from a tree he was climbing, and a child with multiple bruises may be anemic.

Others of these characteristics obviously can only be the result of abuse or neglect: a child who is pregnant or has venereal disease, a child who is hungry or in need of medical attention, a child who has cigarette or cigar burns on his body, and so on. Children who display symptoms which have no possible explanation other than abuse or neglect are in desperate need of immediate assistance.

The key is to use common sense. If your intellect and your instincts tell you that a child is being abused, look for the signs. When several of the indicators are present (and could have no other possible explanation) and your instincts and common sense tell you the child is in danger, you are obligated by all that is decent and right to report your suspicions to those who are in a position to protect the child and assist the family. Look in the front of your telephone directory under emergency numbers or call the information operator to get the number of your local or state domestic violence or child abuse hotline. Call the number and provide whatever information they request, and remember that you may remain anonymous if you wish.

Cases which are less clear-cut require a different approach. Perhaps you are aware of a family in which the parents simply don't know how to respond to a child's many physical, emotional, intellectual, and spiritual needs. Maybe the family is overburdened with financial problems, a terminally ill family member, or some other difficulty which keeps the parents from being the patient and attentive parents they might otherwise be. You can be of significant help to such families and perhaps, in the long run, save a child.

If you are a relative or friend of the child's family or even an acquaintance who is able to approach the family, spend time with them and offer your support and assistance in the way of childcare, donations of food or clothing if they are in need, and contacts with church or civic organizations which can meet other needs the family may have. By spending time with the entire family, you can model parenting skills for the parents by interacting with the child. By offering childcare or outings and activities with the child, you give the parents "cooling off" time. You also have opportunities to observe and talk with the child to determine whether the situation warrants further intervention, and—possibly most important of all—you provide the child with what some child abuse experts call a helping witness or compassionate observer.

This compassionate observer or helping witness is a caring adult who spends time with a child whose other contacts with adults may be abusive or, at the very least, less than positive (this observer or witness may not even be aware that the child is in a less-than-ideal family situation). During this time, the observer or witness lets the child know that she cares about him, thinks he's smart and capable, and believes in him. It may be a neighbor who sits on the front porch and invites the child to sit and chat. It may be a relative who invites the child to spend the weekend and takes him to a baseball game or the circus. It can be anyone who sees a child in need—even if he is just in need of a friend—and reaches out to him.

In *The Untouched Key* (New York: Random House [1990], 159), Alice Miller defined the importance of this person in a child's life when she made the following observation: "The absence or presence of a helping witness in childhood determines whether a mistreated child will become a despot who turns his repressed feelings of helplessness against others or an artist who can tell about his or her suffering."

Other ways in which you can help children who are experiencing domestic violence (suggested by the Centre County Women's Resource Center of Pennsylvania) include encouraging your school system to educate young people about domestic violence and to help them develop abuse-free relationships; teaching young people that physical force is not an acceptable way to solve problems or control other people; and supporting laws that are for the rights of battered women and their children.

It is also incumbent on each of us to protect our own children from abuse. If you are an abused woman with children, please contact your local program for battered women. It is your legal and moral responsibility to protect your children from harm. If you are a parent who is abusing your children, *it is your legal and moral responsibility to stop abusing them.* You can get help by contacting your local domestic violence program and asking for counseling and support. The counselors there will be able to put you in touch with a support group for parents who abuse their children as well as a support group for your children so that they may begin to recover.

Too, we all need to protect our children from the possibility of sexual abuse by talking frankly with them about people who may try to harm them. The following guidelines were published in the *Time-Out Newslet-ter* (Spring/Summer 1991):

• Explain to your children that their bodies be-long only to them and that they have the right to say no to anyone who might try to touch them.

• Tell your children that some adults may try to hurt children and make them do things they don't feel comfortable doing. Often these grownups call what they are doing a "secret" between themselves and the child.

• Explain that some adults may even threaten children by saying that their parents may be hurt or killed if the child ever shares the secret. Emphasize that an adult who does this is doing something very wrong.

• Tell your children that even adults whom they know, trust and love, or someone who might be in a position of authority (baby-sitter, uncle, teacher, po-liceman) might try to do something like this. Try not to scare your children—emphasize that the vast major-ity of grownups never do this and that most adults are deeply concerned about protecting children from harm.

Teen Dating Violence

The facts are staggering:

• Research indicates that violence or threats of violence occur in about 35 percent of teen-age dating couples.

• Violence or threats of violence occur in one out of six relationships between couples in college.

• Dating violence has been experienced by one out of four teen-agers.

• Four thousand women are killed in the United States each year by their husbands *or boyfriends*.

These statistics are especially frightening when you consider that your own teen-age daughter may be the next victim. With that in mind, make a point of sitting down with your daughter to teach her the warning signs. Have her ask herself these questions:

Psychological and emotional abuse—Does he put you down and make you feel bad about yourself? Does he play mind games or make you feel crazy? Does he tell secrets to others? Does he ignore you or give you the silent treatment? Does he blame you when he mistreats you by saying that you provoked him, pushed his buttons, made him do it, or led him on?

Verbal abuse—Does he call you names, criticize you, publicly embarrass or humiliate you?

Destruction of personal property—Does he destroy personal items of yours such as pictures, letters, clothing, or gifts? Does he ruin your belongings, deface or cause damage to your home or automobile?

Threats, anger, and intimidation—Does he use looks, actions, expressions, or a loud voice to intimidate you? Does he smash or throw things to frighten you? Does he threaten to leave you or abandon you in dangerous places? Does he threaten to hurt you physically?

Jealousy, isolation, possessiveness, and restriction of freedoms—Does he use jealousy as a sign of love? Did he come on very strong at the beginning of your relationship and become too serious too fast? Does he control what you do, who you see and talk to, and where you go? Does he refuse to let you work or join activities, or does he drop by to watch you during your activities? Does he accuse you of cheating on him? Does he refuse to accept your breaking up with him?

Abuse of male privilege—Does he make all the decisions? Does he go out with his friends but not allow you to go out with your friends? Does he believe in a double standard which says that boys have certain freedoms which girls do not have? Does he walk out and leave you during arguments? Does he do all the telephoning and expect you to always be there when he calls? Is he very bossy? Does he give you orders? Does he refuse to take your opinions seriously? Does he believe that men should be in control and powerful and that women should be passive and submissive?

Sexual abuse—Does he touch you in ways or in places which you do not want or which make you uncomfortable? Does he continue to make sexual advances after you have told him no? Does he tell you that "you would if you really loved me" or that, if you don't have sex with him, he will have sex with someone else? Does he force you to have sex? Does he make use of playful force during sex? Does he treat you like a sex object?

Physical abuse—Has he made any attempt to hurt or scare you physically? Has he hit or bitten you? Has he pulled your hair? Has he grabbed, pushed, shoved, tripped, or kicked you? Does he own weapons? Is he scary? Does he have a history of fighting or of hitting former girlfriends? If so, does he blame the other person in those fights? Does he abuse drugs or alcohol and pressure you to use them? Have your friends or family members warned you about him or told you they were worried for your safety when you are with him?

If your daughter recognizes that she is in a violent or potentially violent relationship, you can help her get out of it by contacting the local battered women's program and attending counseling and support group sessions with her. Encourage her to bring charges against her abuser (bring charges yourself if she is a minor) if such charges are warranted, and stick by her while she follows through on those charges.

What if your daughter refuses to admit that the relationship is violent or potentially violent, or what if she admits it but refuses to end the relationship? Obviously, if she is a minor, you can take steps to try to prevent her from seeing her abuser again, such as restricting her to the house, refusing to let her receive phone calls from him or make calls to him, and telling him yourself that he is no longer welcome at your home and is not to try to see or contact your daughter in any way. However, such forceful tactics are seldom successful with headstrong teen-agers.

Your best recourse is to contact your local battered women's program and make an appointment with a counselor or advocate. Encourage your daughter to keep the appointment, and go with her; if she refuses, go by yourself and ask the counselor with whom you speak for specific advice to help you help your daughter. Encourage her to attend support group sessions sponsored by the battered women's program or shelter in your community, and go with her. Encourage her to join organizations and to take up activities which do not include her abuser. Help her meet and make new friends. Spend as much time with her as you possibly can. Listen to her and do not judge. Remember that the victim is never to blame for the abuse.

If your daughter is a minor and has been physically or sexually assaulted, you can and must bring charges against her abuser no matter how much she pleads with you not to. Failure to do so may be considered child neglect on your part. Request the assistance of the legal advocate or other counselor at the battered women's program or shelter in your community or contact the district attorney's office.

I have heard of very serious cases in which desperate parents have made the decision to move away from the community in which their daughter's abuser lived or have taken other drastic measures to protect her. Sometimes these measures worked; sometimes they didn't. A teen-age girl in love who does not believe her boyfriend is abusive or who believes she can change him can find her way back to him if she is determined enough. An enraged abuser can track down his victim wherever her family has moved if he is determined enough. The best you can do is to do the best you can.

Follow the guidelines in this book. Give your daughter a copy of this book. Stay in touch with your local battered women's program, and stay in touch with your daughter.

If your daughter is no longer a minor, you will have to approach the situation much like you would if she were a friend, neighbor, co-worker, or other relative. Sadly, we cannot force those we love to do as we say or to take our advice when they are past the age of consent.

How to Help an Adult
Who Is in an Abusive Relationship

When you suspect that an adult you care about is in an abusive relationship, tactfully let her know that you are available if she needs to talk about anything. If she takes you up on your offer, spend your time with her listening. If she skirts the issue of abuse, lead her to it gently, letting her know that her confidences are safe with you and that you will not speak of them to anyone without her permission. Be there for her. For a while, that may be all you are able to do.

If she chooses to talk to you about the violence in her life, tell her about available resources. Offer to help her talk to her family and enlist their support and assistance. Offer to help her make contact with the local battered women's program, a counselor, an attorney, and any other professional she may need to contact and go with her to those appointments. Give her a copy of this book.

If she is in immediate danger, urge her to call the police and to leave and go to a safe place. If she won't or can't call the police, make the call for her.

If she is injured, encourage her to go to the emergency room and go with her. Encourage her to save evidence of physical abuse and to press charges. Go to the police station or magistrate's office with her.

Remember that a woman who has been battered is a victim of a crime, and victims need special support from those who care about them.

• Continue to make yourself available when the victim needs someone to talk to. Remind her that she is not to blame for the abuse. Always be supportive and nonjudgmental.

• Don't tell her how she should or shouldn't feel. It's normal for her to experience a wide range of emotions.

• Be watchful for symptoms which may require medical or psychiatric assistance.

• Be patient. Recovery from abuse has no time-table.

Final thoughts. Someone once told me he believed that when we go to heaven, God asks each of us three questions about our lives: How much did you love? How much did you learn? How is the world a better place because you were there?

All the complex and profound truths of all the great religions and philosophies are right there in those three simple questions, and our answers to those questions are really all that matter when the end comes. If we can answer that we loved unconditionally and reached out to others unfailingly, then the answer to "How much did you learn?" may be "Everything."

Personal Safety Plan

The following personal safety plan was furnished by Sgt. Anne O'Dell, a domestic violence specialist with the San Diego Police Department.

The following steps represent my plan for increasing my safety and preparing in advance for the possibility of further violence. Although I do not have control over my partner's violence, I do have a choice about how to respond to him and how to best get myself and my children to safety.

Step 1: Safety During a Violent Incident. Women cannot always avoid violent incidents. In order to increase safety, battered women may employ a variety of strategies.

I can use some or all of the following strategies:

A. If I decide to leave, I will _____

_____.

(Practice how to get out safely. What doors, windows, elevators, stairwells or fire escapes would you use?)

B. I can keep my purse and car keys ready and put them in (place) _____ in order to leave quickly.

C. I can tell (name someone you trust) _____

_____ about the violence and request they call the police if they hear suspicious noises coming from my house. I can also tell (name a second person you trust) _____ about the violence and request they call the police if they hear suspicious noises coming from my house.

D. I can teach my children how to use the telephone to contact the police and the fire department.

E. I will use _____ as my code word with my children or my friends so they can call for help.

F. If I have to leave my home, I will go _____ _____. (Decide this even if you don't think there will be a next time.) If I cannot go to the location above, then I can go to_____ _____ or to _____ _____.

G. I can also teach some of these strategies to some/all of my children.

H. When I expect my partner and I are going to have an argument, I will try to move to a space that is lowest risk such as _____. (Remember to avoid the bathroom, kitchen, garage, rooms containing weapons and rooms without access to the outside.)

I. I will use my judgment and intuition. If the situation is very serious, I can give my partner what he wants to calm him down. I have to protect myself and the children until we are out of danger.

Step 2: Safety When Preparing to Leave. Battered women frequently leave the residence they share with the battering partner. Leaving must be done strategically in order to increase safety. Batterers often strike back when they believe that a battered woman is leaving the relationship.

I can use some or all of the following safety strategies:

A. I will leave money and an extra set of keys with _____ so I can leave quickly.

B. I will keep copies of important documents at _____.

C. I will open a savings account by _____ (date) in order to increase my independence.

D. Other things I can do to increase my independence include: _____ _____.

E. The domestic violence program's hotline number is _____.

I can seek shelter by calling this number
_____.

F. I can keep change for phone calls on me at all times. I understand that if I use my telephone credit card, the following month the telephone bill will tell my batterer those numbers that I called after I left. To keep my telephone communications confidential, I must either use coins or I might get a friend to permit me to use her telephone credit card for a limited time when I first leave.

G. I will check with _____ and _____ to see who would be able to let me stay with them or lend me some money.

H. I can leave extra clothes with _____
_____.

I. I will sit down and review my safety plan every _____(week? two weeks? month?) in order to plan the safest way to leave the residence. _____
_____(domestic violence advocate or friend) has agreed to help me review this plan.

J. I will rehearse my escape plan and, as appropriate, practice it with my children.

Step 3: Safety in My Own Residence. There are many things that a woman can do to increase her safety in her own residence. It may be impossible to do everything at once, but safety measures can be added step by step.

Safety measures I can use include:

A. I can change the locks on my doors and windows as soon as possible.

B. I can replace wooden doors with steel/metal doors.

C. I can install security systems including additional locks, window bars, poles to wedge against doors, an electronic system, etc.

D. I can purchase rope ladders to be used for escape from second floor windows.

E. I can install smoke detectors and purchase fire extinguishers for each floor in my house/apartment.

F. I can install an outside lighting system that lights up when a person is coming close to my home.

G. I will teach my children how to use the telephone to make a collect call to me and to _____ _____(friend, minister, relative, etc.) in the event that my partner abducts the children.

H. I will tell people who take care of my children which people have permission to pick up my children and that my partner is not permitted to do so. The people I will inform about pick-up permission include:

(school) _____

(daycare staff) _____

(baby-sitter) _____

(Sunday School teacher) _____

(teacher) _____

(others) _____

_____

I. I can inform (neighbor)_____,
(pastor)_____, and
(friend)_____ that my partner no longer resides with me and they should call the police if he is observed near my residence.

Step 4: Safety with a Protection Order. Many batterers obey protection orders, but one can never be sure which violent partner will obey and which will violate protection orders. I recognize that I may need to ask the police and the courts to enforce my protection order.

The following are some steps that I can take to help the enforcement of my protection order:

A. I will keep my protection order (location) _____. (Always keep it on or near your person. If you change purses, that's the first thing that should go in.)

B. I will give my protection order to police departments in the community where I work, in those communities where I usually visit friends or family, and in the community where I live.

C. Some counties keep a registry of protection orders that other police departments can call to confirm the validity of a protection order. I can make sure my order is in the registry. The telephone number for the county registry (Marshall's office) is _____.

D. For further safety, if I often visit other counties, I might file my protection order with the court in those counties. I will register my order in the following counties:

_____

_____.

E. I can call the local domestic violence program if I am not sure about B, C, or D above or if I have some problem with or question about my protection order.

F. I will inform my employer, my minister, my closest friend, and _____

that I have a protection order in effect.

G. If my partner destroys my protection order, I can get another copy from the court located at _____

_____.

H. If my partner violates the protection order, I can call the police and report a violation, contact my attorney, call my advocate, and/or advise the court of the violation.

I. If the police do not help, I can contact my advocate or attorney and will file a complaint with the chief of the police department.

J. I can also file a private criminal complaint with the

_____.

Step 5: Safety on the Job and in Public. Each battered woman must decide if and when she will tell others that her partner has battered her and that she may be at continued risk. Friends, family, and co-workers can help to protect women. Each woman should consider carefully which people to invite to help secure her safety.

I might do any or all of the following:

A. I can inform my boss, the security supervisor, and _____at work of my situation.

B. I can ask _____ to help screen my telephone calls at work.

C. When leaving work, I can_____

_____ to ensure my safety.

D. If problems occur while I am driving home, I can

_____.

E. If I use public transit, I can _____

_____.

F. I can use different grocery stores and shopping malls to conduct my business and shop at hours that are different from those I used when living with my partner.

G. I can also _____

_____.

Step 6: Safety and Drug or Alcohol Consumption. Most people in this culture consume alcohol. Many consume mood-altering drugs. Much of this consumption is legal and some is not. The legal outcomes of using illegal drugs can be very hard on a battered woman, may hurt her relationships with her children, and put her at a disadvantage in other legal actions with her battering partner. Therefore, women should carefully consider the potential cost of the use of illegal drugs. But beyond this, the use of any alcohol and other drugs can reduce a woman's awareness and ability to act quickly to protect herself and her children from the batterer. Furthermore, the use of alcohol or other drugs by the batterer may give him an excuse to use violence. Therefore, in the context of drug or alcohol consumption, a woman needs to make specific safety plans.

If drug or alcohol consumption has occurred in my relationship with the battering partner, I can enhance my safety by some or all of the following:

A. If I am going to consume, I can do so in a safe place and with people who understand the risk of violence and are committed to my safety.

B. I can also _____

_____.

C. If my partner is consuming, I can _____

_____.

D. I might also _____

_____.

E. To safeguard my children, I can _____

_____.

Step 7: Safety and My Emotional Health. The experience of being battered and/or verbally degraded by partners is usually exhausting and emotionally draining. The process of building a new life for yourself takes much courage and incredible energy. To conserve my emotional energy and resources and to avoid hard emotional times, I can do some of the following:

A. If I feel down and ready to return to a potentially abusive situation, I can_____

_____.

B. When I have to communicate with my partner in person or by telephone, I can _____

_____.

C. I can use "I can . . ." statements with myself and be assertive with others.

D. I can tell myself, "_____

_____" when I feel others are trying to control or abuse me.

E. I can read _____to help me feel stronger.

F. I can call _____,

_____, and _____

_____ to be of support to me.

G. Other things I can do to help me feel stronger are

_____, _____, and _____.

H. I can attend workshops and support groups at the domestic violence program or at _____

_____ to gain support and strengthen my relationships with other people.

Step 8: Items to Take When Leaving. When women leave partners, it is important to take certain items with them. Beyond this, women sometimes give an extra copy of papers and an extra set of clothing to a friend just in case they have to leave quickly.

Items with asterisks on the following list are the most important to take. If there is time, the other items might be taken or stored outside the home.

These items might best be placed in one location so that, if we have to leave in a hurry, I can grab them quickly.

When I leave I should take:

* * • Identification for myself
* * • Children's birth certificates
* * • My birth certificate
* * • Social Security cards and my partner's Social Security number
* * • School and vaccination records

* * Money
* * Checkbook, ATM card
* * Credit cards
* * Keys—house, car, office
* * Driver's license and car registration
* * Medications
  * Welfare identification
  * Work permits
  * Green card
  * Passport(s)
  * Divorce papers
  * Medical records—for all family members
  * Lease/rental agreement, house deed, mortgage payment book
  * Bank books
  * Insurance papers
  * Small salable objects
  * Address book
  * Pictures
  * Jewelry
  * Children's favorite toys and/or blankets
  * Items of special sentimental value

Telephone Numbers I Need to Know:

Police, Fire and Rescue—911
Battered Women's Program_____
County Registry of Protection Orders _____
Work Number _____
Supervisor's Home Number _____
Minister _____
_____
_____

Appendix B

Resources for Abused Women

The domestic violence sources listed by state can give you the telephone number of the battered women's shelter and/or program nearest you. The legal organizations can provide information about the laws in your home state and referral to the appropriate advocacy group.

Alabama

Alabama Coalition Against Domestic Violence—(205) 832-4842

Legal Services Corporation of Alabama, Inc.—(205) 264-1471

Alaska

Alaska Network on Domestic Violence and Sexual Assault—(907) 586-3650

Alaska Legal Services Corporation—(907) 276-6282

Arizona

Arizona Coalition Against Domestic Violence—(602) 279-2900 or 1-800-782-6400

Community Legal Services, Inc.—(602) 258-3434

Arkansas

Arkansas Coalition Against Violence to Women and Children—(501) 663-4668

Central Arkansas Legal Services, Inc.—(501) 376-3423

California

California Alliance against Domestic Violence—(209) 524-1888

Legal Aid Foundation of Los Angeles—(213) 964-7950

Colorado

Colorado Domestic Violence Coalition—(303) 573-9018

Legal Aid Society of Metropolitan Denver, Inc.—(303) 837-1313

Connecticut

Connecticut Coalition Against Domestic Violence—(203) 524-5890

Neighborhood Legal Services, Inc.—(203) 297-0760

Delaware

Delaware Coalition Against Domestic Violence—(302) 762-6110

Community Legal Aid Society, Inc.—(302) 575-0660

District of Columbia

DC Coalition Against Domestic Violence—(202) 783-5332

Neighborhood Legal Services Program of the District of Columbia—(202) 682-2720

Florida

Florida Coalition Against Domestic Violence—(904) 668-6862

Legal Services of Greater Miami, Inc.—(305) 576-0080

Georgia

Georgia Advocates for Battered Women and Children—(404)524-3847 or 1-800-643-1212

Georgia Legal Services Program—(404) 656-6021

Hawaii

Hawaii State Committee on Family Violence—(808) 595-3900

Legal Aid Society of Hawaii—(808) 536-4302

Idaho

Idaho Coalition Against Sexual & Domestic Violence—(208) 384-0419

Idaho Legal Aid Services, Inc.—(208) 336-8980

Illinois

Illinois Coalition Against Domestic Violence—(217) 789-2830

Legal Assistance Foundation of Chicago—(312) 341-1070

Indiana

Indiana Coalition Against Domestic Violence—(317) 543-3908

Legal Services Organization of Indiana, Inc.—(317) 631-9410

Iowa

Iowa Coalition Against Domestic Violence—(515) 281-7284

Legal Services Corporation of Iowa—(515) 243-2151

Kansas

Kansas Coalition Against Sexual and Domestic Violence—(913) 232-9784

Kansas Legal Services, Inc.—(913) 233-2068

Kentucky

Kentucky Domestic Violence Association—(502) 875-4132

Legal Aid Society, Inc.—(502) 584-1254

Louisiana

Louisiana Coalition Against Domestic Violence—(504) 542-4446

Louisiana Legal Consortium, Inc.—(504) 924-5524

Maine

Maine Coalition for Family Crisis Services—(207) 941-1194

Pine Tree Legal Assistance, Inc.—(207) 774-4753

Maryland

Maryland Network Against Domestic Violence—(301) 942-0900

Legal Aid Bureau, Inc.—(410) 539-5340

Massachusetts

Massachusetts Coalition of Battered Women's Service Groups—(617) 248-0922

Volunteer Lawyers Project of the Boston Bar Association, Inc.—(617) 423-0648

Michigan

Michigan Coalition Against Domestic Violence—(517) 484-2924

Michigan Legal Services—(313) 964-4130

Minnesota

Minnesota Coalition For Battered Women—(612) 646-6177

Legal Aid Service of Northeastern Minnesota—(218) 726-4800

Mississippi

Mississippi Coalition Against Domestic Violence—(601) 436-3809

Central Mississippi Legal Services—(601) 948-6752

Missouri

Missouri Coalition Against Domestic Violence—(314) 634-4161

Legal Aid of Western Missouri—(816) 474-6750

Montana

Montana Coalition Against Domestic Violence—(406) 586-7689

Montana Legal Services Association—(406) 442-9830

Nebraska

Nebraska Domestic Violence and Sexual Assault Coalition—(402) 476-6256

Legal Aid Society, Inc.—(402) 348-1060

Nevada

Nevada Network Against Domestic Violence—(702) 358-1171 or 1-800-500-1556 (state hotline)

Nevada Legal Services, Inc.—(702) 386-1070

New Hampshire

New Hampshire Coalition Against Domestic Violence & Sexual Violence—(603) 224-8893 or 1-800-852-3388 (state hotline)

New Hampshire Legal Assistance, Inc.—(603) 225-4700

New Jersey

New Jersey Coalition for Battered Women—(609) 584-8107 or 1-800-572-7233 (state hotline)

Legal Services of New Jersey, Inc.—(908) 572-9100

New Mexico

New Mexico State Coalition Against Domestic Violence— (505) 246-9240 or 1-800-773-3645

Legal Aid Society of Albuquerque, Inc.—(505) 243-7871

New York

New York State Coalition Against Domestic Violence—(518) 432-4864 or 1-800-942-6906 (English) or 1-800-942-6908 (Spanish)

The Legal Aid Society/Volunteer Division—(212) 577-3300

North Carolina

North Carolina Coalition Against Domestic Violence—(919) 490-1467

Legal Services of North Carolina, Inc.—(919) 856-2121

North Dakota

North Dakota Council on Abused Women's Services—(701) 255-6240 or 1-800-472-2911 (state hotline)

Legal Assistance of North Dakota, Inc.—(701) 222-2110

Ohio

Action Ohio Coalition for Battered Women—(614) 221-1255 or 1-800-934-9840

Ohio Domestic Violence Network—(614) 784-0023

Ohio State Legal Services—(614) 299-2114

Oklahoma

Oklahoma Coalition on Domestic Violence & Sexual Assault— (405) 557-1210 or 1-800-522-9054

Legal Aid of Western Oklahoma, Inc.—(405) 557-0020

Oregon

Oregon Coalition Against Domestic Violence—(503) 223-7411

Oregon Legal Services Corporation—(503) 234-1534

Pennsylvania

Pennsylvania Coalition Against Domestic Violence—(717) 545-6400 or 1-800-932-4632 (state hotline)
Legal Services, Inc.—(717) 334-7623

Puerto Rico

Commission Para Los Asuntos—(809) 722-2907
Puerto Rico Legal Services, Inc.—(809) 728-8686

Rhode Island

Rhode Island Council on Domestic Violence—(401) 723-3051
Rhode Island Legal Services, Inc.—(401) 274-2652

South Carolina

South Carolina Coalition Against Domestic Violence & Sexual Assault—(803) 254-3699
Carolina Regional Legal Services Corporation—(803) 667-1896

South Dakota

South Dakota Coalition Against Domestic Violence & Sexual Assault—(605) 225-5122
East River Legal Services—(605) 336-9230

Tennessee

Tennessee Task Force Against Family Violence—(615) 327-0805 or 1-800-356-6767 (state hotline)
Knoxville Legal Aid Society, Inc.—(615) 637-0484

Texas

Texas Council on Family Violence—(512) 794-1133
Texas Legal Services Center—(512) 477-6000

Utah

Utah Domestic Violence Advisory Council—(801) 538-4100
Utah Legal Services, Inc.—(801) 328-8891

Vermont

Vermont Network Against Domestic Violence & Sexual Assault—(802) 223-1302
Vermont Legal Aid, Inc.—(802) 863-5620

U.S. Virgin Islands

St. Croix—(809) 773-9272
St. Thomas/St. John—(809) 776-3966
Legal Services of the Virgin Islands, Inc.—(809) 773-2626

Virginia

Virginians Against Domestic Violence—(804) 221-0990 or 1-800-838-8238
Virginia Legal Aid Society, Inc.—(804) 528-4722

Washington

Washington State Coalition Against Domestic Violence—(206) 352-4029 or 1-800-562-6025 (state hotline)
Evergreen Legal Services—(206) 464-5933

West Virginia

West Virginia Coalition Against Domestic Violence—(304) 765-2250
West Virginia Legal Services Plan, Inc.—(304) 342-6814

Wisconsin

Wisconsin Coalition Against Domestic Violence—(608) 255-0539
Legal Action of Wisconsin, Inc.—(414) 278-7777

Wyoming

Wyoming Coalition Against Domestic Violence & Sexual Assault—(307) 235-2814
Legal Aid Services, Inc.—(307) 235-2786

Other Resources

National Council on Child Abuse and Family Violence
1155 Connecticut Avenue, NW
Suite 400
Washington, D.C. 20036
(202) 429-6695

Center for the Prevention of Sexual and Domestic Violence
1914 North 34th Street, Suite 105
Seattle, WA 98103
(206) 634-1903

Specialized Training on Preventing Domestic Violence (STOP DV)

National Headquarters
750 State Street, Suite 307
San Diego, California 92101
(619) 236-9733

National Coalition Against Domestic Violence
P.O. Box 18749
Denver, CO 80218
(303) 839-1852

National Clearinghouse for the Defense of Battered Women
125 South 9th Street, Suite 302
Philadelphia, PA 19107
(215) 351-0010

Military Family Clearinghouse
4015 Wilson Boulevard, #903
Arlington, VA 22203
(703) 696-5860
1-800-336-4592
DSN 226-5806

National Organization for Victim Assistance
1757 Park Road, N.W.
Washington, D.C. 20010
1-800-TRY- NOVA

Project: Protect
P.O. Box 31124
Chicago, Illinois 60631
1-800-380-4888

Centre County Women's Resource Center
140 W. Nittany Avenue.
State College, Pennsylvania 16801
(814) 234-5222

Information Plus
2812 Exchange Street
Wylie, Texas 75098

We welcome comments from our readers. Feel free to write to us at the following address:

Editorial Department
Huntington House Publishers
P.O. Box 53788
Lafayette, LA 70505

======

More Good Books from Huntington House

Homeless in America: The Solution
by Jeremy Reynalds

Author Jeremy Reynalds' current shelter, Joy Junction, located in Albuquerque, New Mexico, has become the state's largest homeless shelter. Beginning with fifty dollars in his pocket and a lot of compassion, Jeremy Reynalds now runs a shelter that has a yearly budget of over $600,000. He receives no government or United Way funding. Anyone who desires to help can, says Reynalds. If you feel a burden to help those less fortunate than you, read this book.

ISBN 1-56384-063-4

ORDER THESE HUNTINGTON HOUSE BOOKS

- *Anyone Can Homeschool*—Terry Dorian & Zan Peters Tyler
- *The Assault*—Dale A. Berryhill
- *Beyond Political Correctness*—David Thibodaux
- *The Best of HUMAN EVENTS*—Edited by James C. Roberts
- *Bleeding Hearts and Propaganda*—James R. Spencer
- *Can Families Survive in Pagan America?*—Samuel Dresner
- *Circle of Death*—Richmond Odom
- *Children No More*—Brenda Scott
- *Combat Ready*—Lynn Stanley
- *Conservative, American & Jewish*—Jacob Neusner
- *The Dark Side of Freemasonry*—Ed Decker
- *The Demonic Roots of Globalism*—Gary Kah
- *Do Angels Really Exist?*—David O. Dykes
- *En Route to Global Occupation*—Gary Kah
- *Everyday Evangelism*—Ray Comfort
- **Exposing the AIDS Scandal*—Dr. Paul Cameron
- *Freud's War with God*—Jack Wright, Jr.
- *Gays & Guns*—John Eidsmoe
- *Global Bondage*—Cliff Kincaid
- *Goddess Earth*—Samantha Smith
- *Health Begins in Him*—Terry Dorian
- *Heresy Hunters*—Jim Spencer
- *Hidden Dangers of the Rainbow*—Constance Cumbey
- *High-Voltage Christianity*—Michael Brown
- *High on Adventure*—Stephen Arrington
- *Homeless in America*—Jeremy Reynalds
- *How to Homeschool (Yes, You!)*—Julia Toto
- *Hungry for God*—Larry E. Myers
- *I Shot an Elephant in My Pajamas*—Morrie Ryskind w/ John Roberts
- **Inside the New Age Nightmare*—Randall Baer
- *A Jewish Conservative Looks at Pagan America*—Don Feder
- *Journey into Darkness*—Stephen Arrington
- *Kinsey, Sex and Fraud*—Dr. Judith A. Reisman & Edward Eichel
- *The Liberal Contradiction*—Dale A. Berryhill
- *Legalized Gambling*—John Eidsmoe
- *The Media Hates Conservatives*—Dale A. Berryhill
- *New Gods for a New Age*—Richmond Odom
- *One Man, One Woman, One Lifetime*—Rabbi Reuven Bulka
- *Out of Control*—Brenda Scott
- *Outcome-Based Education*—Peg Luksik & Pamela Hoffecker
- *The Parched Soul of America*—Leslie Kay Hedger w/ Dave Reagan
- *Please Tell Me*—Tom McKenney
- *Political Correctness*—David Thibodaux
- *Resurrecting the Third Reich*—Richard Terrell
- *Revival: Its Principles and Personalities*—Winkie Pratney

*Available in Salt Series

Available at bookstores everywhere or order direct from:
Huntington House Publishers • P.O. Box 53788 • Lafayette, LA 70505
Call toll-free 1-800-749-4009